Studies in Political Science

Edited by MALCOLM ANDERSON

I

POLITICAL REPRESENTATION
AND ELECTIONS

STUDIES IN POLITICAL SCIENCE

British Government

The Prime Minister and the Cabinet
  by J. P. Mackintosh
The Legislative Process in Great Britain
  by S. A. Walkland
The British Constitution
  by P. Bromhead
The Making of Defence Policy
  by J. A. Sabine
The Making of British Foreign Policy
  by David Vital
Opinions, Publics and Pressure Groups
  by Graeme C. Moodie
Politics and Planning
  by L. A. Gunn
Politics and Education
  by J. R. Brand

Comparative Government

The New French Parliament
  by Philip Williams
Soviet Local Government
  by Jennie Chapman
Political Elites
  by G. B. Parry
The Politics of Protest
  by David Goldey
Church and State
  by A. C. Gough
Civil Liberties
  by D. T. G. Williams
The Gaullist Movement in the Fifth Republic
  by Jean Charlot

Further titles to be announced

POLITICAL REPRESENTATION AND ELECTIONS

Parties and Voting in Great Britain

Peter G. J. Pulzer

FREDERICK A. PRAEGER, *Publishers*
NEW YORK · WASHINGTON

Published in the United States of America in 1967
by Frederick A. Praeger, Inc., Publishers
111 Fourth Avenue, New York, N.Y. 10003

This book is published in Great Britain as
Political Representation and Elections in Britain

Library of Congress Catalog Card Number: 67- 28784

Printed in Great Britain

FOR GILLIAN

PREFACE

In the past twenty years the study and conduct of elections in Britain have undergone a minor revolution. Thanks mainly to the election studies sponsored by Nuffield College, Oxford, and the increasing reliability of opinion polls we know much more than we did about how people vote and why. This knowledge has, in turn, affected the methods and assumptions of our political leaders, and the techniques of public relations have, however uncertainly and inconsistently entered British election campaigns.

I have aimed in this book at summarizing the present state of knowledge in these matters, up to and including the General Election of 1966. Since this new knowledge also raises important questions concerning the rôle and value of our representative institutions, and the place of elections in the representative system, I have supplemented the narrative portions of the book with a formulation of these questions and an attempt to suggest answers to them.

Britain is an island geographically, and to some extent politically. Much in our present-day political institutions must be understood in terms of the historical development of Parliament and its struggle with the crown. I have tried to do justice to this, and at the same time place our present-day experience in its international context by drawing on the most recent research in other Western countries.

I am grateful to Dr Malcolm Anderson, of the University of Warwick, and Mr Philip Williams, of Nuffield College, Oxford, for reading the manuscript and making numerous helpful suggestions. They bear no responsibility, of course, for any remaining solecisms. I am also grateful to Dr J. F. A. Mason, Librarian of Christ Church, for his meticulous reading of the proofs.

Dr J. G. Blumler, Granada Fellow of the Television Research Unit, University of Leeds, and Mr Williams kindly let me see the manuscript of forthcoming publications. Both Gallup Poll and the National Opinion Poll kindly supplied data which would otherwise have been difficult to trace.

Oxford, February 1967   PETER G. J. PULZER

CONTENTS

Parliament and Democracy

'IN democratic states,' wrote Aristotle, 'the people (i.e. demos) is sovereign.'[1] Yet it is one thing to possess a legal right, another to exercise it effectively. In Britain we have a Parliament, and parliamentary elections, as instruments for expressing popular opinion democratically. But the day-to-day business of legislation and policy-making, even the organization of the political parties which canalize opinion, is delegated to a small number of representatives elected for that purpose. Clearly there is a point at which democratic purpose and representative institutions may clash; it has been frequently pointed out that the two not only have widely divergent historical origins, but purposes inconsistent with each other. Representation need not be democratic and democracies need not be parliamentary.

REPRESENTATION WITHOUT DEMOCRACY

Parliaments are a legacy of the feudal Middle Ages. Mediaeval monarchs could not expect to rule as autocrats or despots. They were expected to seek the advice of the 'estates of the realm', each of which had defined functions and status, both in relation to each other and in relation to the monarch. Because of poor communications, if for no other reason, monarchs depended on the good-will of local notables for administration, the dispensing of justice, the raising of soldiers and the collection of taxes. Those whose help was indispensable to the monarch were in turn able to insist that the law be not changed, nor taxes levied, without their consent. In England the parliaments which date from the second half of the thirteenth century were representative in two distinct ways, by interest and by territory.

The interests represented in Parliament were the Lords Spiritual (archbishops, bishops and mitred abbots), the Lords Temporal, a category whose definition was uncertain at least until the Tudors, and the Commons. Within the Commons representation was divided between counties and boroughs. Because members of the House of Commons sat on behalf of communities, not interests or individuals, there was no attempt to equate representation with either population of the size of the electorate. Each county sent two knights, each borough two burgesses. The only exception was the City of London which sent four. Within each county the franchise belonged, from 1430, to all freeholders whose tenements had an annual value of 40 shillings. Within the boroughs it varied widely. Neither system was changed until the Reform Act of 1832. By the accession of Henry VIII (1509) the House of Lords numbered about 100, with spiritual peers slightly in the majority. In the Commons 37 counties were represented by 74 members and 110 boroughs by 222 members.[2]

Parliament, like so many other British institutions, nowadays serves purposes far removed from those for which it was originally intended. Yet vestiges of these purposes remain. We still have a House of Lords and a House of Commons. A peer of the realm may not vote in a parliamentary election. A clergyman of the Established Church may not sit in the House of Commons. Each belongs to an 'estate' already represented elsewhere.

But a reminder of the feudal origins of parliamentary representation is not merely of antiquarian interest. Extreme democrats claim that only 'the people' as a whole, undistracted by class interests or party divisions, should exercise sovereignty; doctrinaire liberals that only individual citizens can be properly represented. But mediaeval social theory viewed society 'corporatively' and 'pluralistically'. Each individual belonged in turn to a larger grouping according to his function, occupation or class. Each of these groupings had legitimate, though limited, rights and privileges within society, thus ensuring the cohesion and stability of the whole. This mediaeval corporatist ideal has again become fashionable in the last hundred years and has attracted social reformers who see in it a remedy for the materialism and class warfare of modern industrial society. On the Left it has been the basis for syndicalists and Guild Socialists, who feel that a 'workers' state', with all that this implies in centralization and bureaucracy, is a contradiction in terms. On the Right, where social cohesion and the maintenance (or revival) of traditions are valued more, it has been the basis of a number of Papal encyclicals and of some experiments by Fascist régimes.

Such views are nevertheless a long way from those which dominate the parliamentary and electoral politics of modern Britain. Only during the last three hundred years, since the Restoration of Charles II, has the public discussion about parliament and representation been conducted in a vocabulary whose meanings we readily understand.

In the eighteenth century, under the influence of Whig ideas, it was considered proper and desirable that representation should be by interest, even if these interests were no longer the corporations and estates of mediaeval society. The 'balanced constitution' of the eighteenth century was, in the eyes of its advocates, a balance of the country's most important interests, 'the great peers, the leading landed gentlemen, the opulent merchants and manufacturers, the substantial yeomanry', as Edmund Burke enumerated them.[3] An even more eloquent panegyric of the old system came from Sir Robert Inglis in 1832, during the debate on the Reform Bill. He saw Parliament as

'the only constituent body that ever existed, which comprehends within itself, those who can urge the wants and defend the claims of the landed, the commercial and the professional classes of the country; those who are bound to uphold the prerogatives of the Crown, the privileges of the nobility, the interests of the lower classes, . . . the rights of the distant dependencies, of the East Indies, of the West Indies, of the colonies, of the great corporations'.[4]

All representation of interests presupposes that some interests are more important than others. The Duke of Wellington noted with approval that, 'the representation of the people at present contains a larger body of the property of the country, in which the landed interests have a preponderating influence'.[5] Between 1660 and 1832 Parliament did indeed represent landed property *par excellence*. But it was not merely property collectively, it was also individual property that was represented. According to Namier the great families and the Crown between them were able, in 1760, to nominate nearly half the House of Commons.[6] The Duke of Norfolk alone 'returned' eleven members.

From the end of the eighteenth century onwards this system was subject to criticism from two sources. There were, firstly, those who denied that the balance of interests represented in Parliament corresponded with the balance of interests in the country. The land and, to a limited degree, commerce had spokesmen in Parliament. Manufacturing industry had virtually none. Manchester, Birmingham, Leeds and Glasgow did not return a single member. On these grounds alone at least a radical redistribution of constituencies was demanded. But objections went further. The whole idea that only well-established corporate interest should have a voice in Parliament was being questioned. In its place arose the demand that since it was individual citizens who voted in elections, they should be represented as individuals. It was nonsensical that a taxpayer in one borough should have a free say in who became his MP, while a similar taxpayer in another borough was deprived of it. The logical end of this line of argument was universal suffrage. Under the impact of the American and French revolutions, but spurred also by such domestic events as the attempt to unseat John Wilkes after his election as MP for Middlesex, radical propagandists and radical associations began increasingly to demand suffrage reform. Joseph Priestley, Richard Price and above all Tom Paine based their arguments on human equality and natural rights.[7] Yet one did not have to accept the revolutionary implications of these doctrines in order to advocate 'freer' representation. It was simply necessary to argue that each man was the best guardian of his own interest. Each man should therefore be free to make his political choice without the intervention of patrons and unhampered by the accidental survival of anomalies. This argument belonged to the Utilitarian school, particularly James Mill and Jeremy Bentham. Because it was based on enlightened self-interest rather than radical egalitarianism it was less dangerous to the established order.

Both Bentham and the elder Mill favoured universal suffrage, but this was by no means a necessary consequence of the individualist approach. All that was necessary was that every elector, once the qualifications for the franchise had been consistently defined, should make his personal, unfettered choice. There was no inherent reason why the franchise should not be restricted to taxpayers, property owners, heads of families, or men over 30—to persons, that is, who could be expected to behave in a sober, responsible way—as long as the categories were defined by rational argument rather than historical accident.

When reform did come, it made concessions to each of these criticisms of the old order, but the concession was in each case incomplete. The Reform Act of 1832 did two things. It redistributed constituencies and it extended the right to vote. In redistributing constituencies the Act met the criticism that the country's main interests were unfairly represented. Scotland, Ireland and the North of England gained seats, the South of England lost. Cornwall went down from 42 to 13 seats, Wiltshire from 34 to 18. Lancashire went up from 14 to 28, Staffordshire from 10 to 17. Beyond that there was no attempt to make constituencies of equal size. There were still thirty boroughs with electorates below 300 and twelve with electorates over 5,000.

In dealing with the franchise the Act moved decisively towards individualism. There had already been an important step in this direction in 1828-9, when Catholics and Dissenters were at last given the same political rights (including the right to sit in Parliament) as members of the Church of England.* Now the franchise in all counties and all boroughs was equalized. In the boroughs the right to vote was

*But Jews were excluded until 1858, and atheists until 1888.

given to every householder who occupied a house of at least £10 rental value; in the counties three further categories of copyholders, lease-holders and tenants-at-will were added to the existing forty-shilling freeholders. In some ways the new franchise was more difficult to defend than the old. The old, however eccentric, was at least part of the British way of life. The new invented an arbitrary and not necessarily equitable dividing-line. Sir Robert Peel, leading the Tory opposition to the Bill, asked

'... if it be a question of right, why ... limit the franchise to particular districts and particular classes? Why confine the privilege of voting to those who rent a house at 10 *l.* a year? The law knows no distinction in this respect between the contributors to the support of the state.'

Why exclude 'all that class of society which is above pauperism and below the arbitrary and impassable line of 10 *l.* rental which you have selected?'[8]

Why indeed?

In 1832 British parliamentary representation, feudal and corporative in origin, took an irreversible, but incomplete, step towards democracy, with its urban classical roots.

DEMOCRACY WITHOUT REPRESENTATION

Not only the idea of democracy, but the word itself, came to us from the city-states of classical Greece. But Aristotle's definition of democratic states, that in them 'the people is sovereign', leaves two important questions unsolved. The first is: are 'the people' simply a collection of all the individuals in a state, or are they a cohesive group with common interests and common desires? The second is: how is popular sovereignty to be expressed? Should the whole body of citizens take all the important administrative and judicial decisions, or should these be delegated? And if delegated, how?

Those who advocate pure or direct democracy reply that the people are indeed a collectivity with a will of their own, and that the expression of this will must be protected against two enemies—either self-seeking individuals among the people, or elected representatives who develop autocratic habits. If the people tolerate factions among themselves, or delegate their collective sovereign power to individuals, then there is a danger that this power will slip out of their hands altogether. Among modern political theorists Jean-Jacques Rousseau is the foremost exponent of this doctrine:

B

'Sovereignty, being no more than the exercise of the general will, can never be *alienated*, and . . . the sovereign, who is a collective being only, can be represented by no one but himself . . .

For the same reason that sovereignty is inalienable, so, too, it is *indivisible*. Either the will is general or it is not. Either it is the will of the whole body of the People, or it is the will merely of one section. Sovereignty cannot be *represented*, for the same reason that it cannot be alienated. It consists essentially of the general will, and will cannot be represented . . . The Deputies of the People are not, nor can they be, its representatives. They can only be its Commissioners. They can make no definite decisions. Laws which the People have not ratified in their own person are null and void.'⁹

The argument is simple: those who have the power to make major decisions on behalf of the people, even if freely elected to such positions of power, inevitably become masters, perhaps even tyrants. Parliaments, therefore, can never be democratic and Rousseau had nothing but contempt for the Englishman's 'freedom':

'The English people think that they are free, but in this belief they are profoundly wrong. They are free only when they are electing members of Parliament. Once the election has been completed, they revert to a condition of slavery: they are nothing.'¹⁰

One further consequence follows. If the people's interest is to be opposed to that of individuals it must also be opposed to that of factions. Partisanship belongs to the parliamentary game; partisanship is the expression of special, and therefore selfish, interests. 'If, then, the general will is to be truly expressed, according to Rousseau, it is essential that there be no subsidiary groups within the state.'¹¹ No parliaments, no parties. That, necessarily, is the slogan of all extreme democrats. No power may be interposed between the will of the people and the making of policy. The slogan is valid only if we share two of the extreme democrat's basic assumptions. The first is that all élites and all oligarchies are hostile to the public interest; the second that there can never be any serious dispute as to where the interests of the people lie. The need to take political power out of the hands of 'the interests' or organized minorities, and restore it to 'the people' has been a constant refrain in radical and democratic propaganda over the past two hundred years. It took overtly anti-parliamentary forms most frequently in those states which were least accustomed to the workings of a representative system. Nearly a century after Rousseau the French Socialist, Victor Considérant, thundered:

'If the people delegate their sovereignty, they resign it. The people no longer govern themselves; they are governed ... Then, people, resign your sovereignty! I guarantee you a fate the opposite of Saturn's: your sovereignty will be devoured by your daughter, the Delegation.'[12]

Similar themes recur in Spain, Italy and Russia. In Britain, too, the tendency to equate the will of the people with the public interest was widespread. The Radical J. A. Roebuck, attacking the opponents of working-class suffrage in 1859, claimed

'The majority of a country can have no interest inimical to the interests of the country. If you give power to a minority, that minority may have interests at variance with the interests of the country; but the majority cannot—if they understand their own interests.'[13]

These doctrines, or at least their relevance to modern life, have not lacked critics. The first and most obvious line of attack is that direct participatory democracy may be fine in a Greek city-state or a rural Swiss canton, but it is inapplicable to modern states with fifty or a hundred million inhabitants. To that some anarchists and federalists reply that this merely proves the need to decentralize power and to reduce the size of the unit of administration. It is, indeed, worth noting that the whole idea of a community based on direct self-government is agrarian or at any rate pre-industrial, and that in Western Europe the appeal of such theories has declined since the mid-nineteenth century. In industrial civilization the division of labour is the criterion of modernity in both economic and political processes.

There are, however, three weightier objections to doctrines of primitive democracy. The first is theoretical and it concerns the very nature and definability of such concepts as 'the people'. This objection is discussed later in the book.* The second is technical and is in its essence the subject of a significant admission by Rousseau himself:

'If we take the term in its strict meaning, no true democracy has ever existed, nor ever will. It is against the natural order that a large number should rule and a small number be ruled. It is inconceivable that the people should be in permanent session for the administration of pub-

*See below, pp. 133-4.

lic affairs, and it is clear that commissions could not be set up for that purpose without the form of the administration being thereby changed.'[14]

The most important objection, however, is the third. This challenges not the feasibility of direct democracy, but its desirability. Just as some denounce representative institutions because these interpose an élite between the people and the exercise of power, so others welcome such institutions for precisely this reason. All forms of parliamentary representation modify or qualify the degree to which the wishes or opinions of the governed can influence the policies of the governors. There is, however, an enormous range within which a representative body *can* assert its autonomy.

REPRESENTATIVE DEMOCRACY

The basis characteristics of democracy have not changed since they were defined by Aristotle:

'The law declares equality to mean that the poor are to count no more than the rich: neither is to be sovereign, and both are to be on a level ... A constitution of this kind is bound to be a democracy; for the people are the majority, and the will of the majority is sovereign.'[15]

This definition leaves untouched the question of representative institutions. Extreme democrats reject all representation as being incompatible with popular sovereignty; in the context of nineteenth-century Britain, however, it was the composition, rather than the idea of Parliament itself, that was attacked. Democracy meant, in effect, parliamentary government with universal suffrage and majority rule. Thus the People's Charter, drawn up in 1838 by Radicals dissatisfied with the First Reform Act, made six demands:

'manhood suffrage
secret ballot
payment for members of parliament
abolition of the property qualification for members
equal-sized constituencies
annual elections'

The Chartists seemed to their contemporaries dangerous revolutionaries, but had the Charter been enacted, Rousseau would still have regarded Englishmen as slaves. On the one hand nineteenth-century democrats, whether Radicals like the Chartists, or Utilitarians like Bentham and the elder Mill, were individualists. They were convinced that every sane, adult citizen had the right to a say in the country's government, and to be elected as the representative of his fellow-citizens. At the same time there was a populist element in their thought. Universal suffrage would enfranchise not only every individual, but 'the people', the under-privileged many, collectively. Individual rights were equated with popular sovereignty at the expense of considerable conceptual confusion.* When, after the Reform Act of 1885, the majority of adult males had the vote in Britain, Joseph Chamberlain exclaimed, 'At last we have a Government of the people and by the people'.[16] We are back at Roebuck's insistence that the interests of the majority and the interests of the nation necessarily coincide.

In the twentieth century such self-confident over-simplifications are treated with disdain, and the weaknesses of the classical individualist and populistic standpoints are generally accepted.** There remains one rather more intractable problem. Granted some degree of majority suffrage, how does this affect the position of the individual legislator? Which deserves higher priority—the will of the people, or the MP with a mind of his own?

THE DEMOCRATIC REPRESENTATIVE

Tom Paine, at the end of the eighteenth century, was fully aware of the dilemma and in no doubt as to how it should be resolved. So that

'*the elected* might never form to themselves an interest separate from the electors, prudence will point out the propriety of having elections often; because as the *elected* might by that means return and mix again with the general body of the *electors* in a few months, their fidelity to the public will be secured by the prudent reflection of not making a rod for themselves.'[17]

It was for the same reason that the Chartists demanded annual Parliaments. There were, however, other views on the extent to which

*The two concepts tend also to be confused in R. A. Dahl's otherwise admirable *A Preface to Democratic Theory* (Chicago, 1956), especially p. 45. Dahl regards the majoritarian principle as the most extreme form of democracy, classifying it as 'populistic' (pp. 34–5), but he fails to make the important distinction between extreme populists, who oppose all mediation by representative institutions, and those majoritarians who accept parliamentary forms and who are therefore closer to Dahl's notion of 'limited government'.

**See below, pp. 133-4.

Parliament as a body, and the individual member of it, should be bound by the views and instructions of the electorate. Parliament consisted of the King's advisers. Through Parliament, 'the grand inquest of the nation', grievances might be aired and requests made known. Parliament might participate in the responsibility of governing and might even in the course of time seize the major share of 'carrying on the King's government'; but it needed to do so in the light of the national interest and its own sense of responsibility, not as an unquestioning reflector of the popular mood.

This notion appealed most easily to Tories, to whom national unity and the dignity of the state, personified by the monarch, came paramount. But while the Whigs attached greater importance to Parliament than the Tories, and less to the Crown, they agreed that members of Parliament were responsible primarily to their own consciences. One of them in 1734 declared

'After we are chosen and have taken our seats in the house, we have no longer any dependence on the electors, at least in so far as regards our behaviour here. Their whole power is then devolved upon us, and we are in every question that comes before this House, to regard only the public good in general, and to determine them according to our own judgments.'[18]

It was not merely Parliament collectively, but the individual MP also, who was considered autonomous. The classical claim on behalf of the independent parliamentarian was that made by Edmund Burke to the electors of Bristol after the declaration of the poll in 1774:

'Parliament is not a *congress* of ambassadors from different and hostile interests; ... but parliament is a *deliberative* assembly of *one* nation, with *one* interest, that of the whole ... You choose a member indeed; but when you have chosen him, he is not member of Bristol, but he is a member of *parliament* ...

Certainly, gentlemen, it ought to be the happiness and glory of a representative to live in the strictest union, the closest correspondence, the most unreserved communication with his constituents ... It is his duty to sacrifice his repose, his pleasures, his satisfactions to theirs. But his unbiased opinion, his enlightened conscience, he ought not to sacrifice to you; to any man, or to any set of men living. These he does not derive from your pleasure; no, nor from the law and the constitution. They are a trust from Providence, for the abuse of which he is deeply answerable. Your representative owes you, not his industry only, but his judgment; and he betrays, instead of serving you, if he sacrifices it to your opinion.'[19]

Such statements, like any other clear-cut attempt at imposing rigorous principle on British constitutional conventions, ignore the compromises and ambiguities of the political market-place. And it may also be said that such lofty, even arrogant, claims to independence are irrelevant in our days of universal suffrage. Yet the notion that 'any set of men living' should be the dictators of an MP's behaviour remains repulsive—at any rate if that set of men are not themselves MPs. When Mr Frank Cousins resigned from the Cabinet in July 1966, and resumed his post as General Secretary of the Transport and General Workers' Union, the union's general council asked him to resign from Parliament. A Liberal MP, quoting Burke's 1774 speech, claimed that the union's action was an attempt to 'control or limit [Mr Cousins'] complete freedom of action in Parliament'. The Speaker rejected the complaint, but only because it had not been raised at the earliest opportunity. He did not pronounce on its merits.[20]

Nor were eighteenth-century claims to independence strictly accurate, since at least half the members of the House of Commons were not 'elected' at all. They were nominated by a patron, and the practice was certainly not an eighteenth-century innovation. The system of patronage did, however, contribute towards making the House of Commons a national forum, as opposed to 'a congress of ambassadors'. While MPs could not avoid speaking and voting for specific economic interests, they could in many cases avoid the concentration on parochial issues which a numerous electorate might have forced on them. There was little pressure on the MP to be a native or a resident of the constituency he sat for. The fifteenth-century statute requiring knights and baronets to be 'dwelling and resident' was soon ignored, though not formally repealed until 1774.[21] According to Sir John Neale at least 164 out of 341 borough members of the 1584 House of Commons were 'outsiders'.[22] Patrons could use their power to advance a brilliant protégé with no local connections. Hampden, the elder and younger Pitt, Fox, Burke, Canning and Gladstone all owed the beginnings of their careers to such 'pocket' or 'rotten' boroughs.

With the extension of the franchise, the question of the member's independence became more, not less acute. Just as Paine and the other radicals saw in the electorate's control over the member a guarantee of democracy, so the more moderate Liberals saw in a strong, independent Parliament a protection against mob rule. To ensure good government, those who compose Parliament must be different from, and better than, the general run of men. They must *not* be representative of the electorate in the sense of being its mirror-image in intellect and social composition. How can this be made to happen? It is possible that the bulk of the electorate actually prefers to be ruled by its betters. Nations where that happens were classified by Walter Bagehot as 'deferential':

'It has been thought strange, but there *are* nations in which the numerous unwiser part wishes to be ruled by the less numerous wiser part. The numerical majority—whether by custom or by choice is immaterial—is ready, is eager to delegate its power of choosing its ruler to a certain select minority. It abdicates in favour of its *élite*, and consents to obey whoever that *élite* may confide in . . .
England is the type of deferential countries.[23]

The mass of the old electors [he wrote some years later, after the Second Reform Act] did not analyze very much: they liked to have one of their 'betters' represent them; if he was rich they respected him much; and if he was a lord they liked him the better. The issue put before these electors was, Which of two rich people will you choose?'[24]

Much has been made of the alleged political deference of the British. Bagehot thought that it was to wealth, social station and public ceremony. More serious-minded Liberals felt that it ought to be to intellect. James Mill, while advocating universal suffrage, was 'perfectly confident' that

'the opinions of that class of the people, who are below the middle rank, are formed and their minds are directed by that intelligent and virtuous rank who come the most immediately into contact with them . . . The vast majority would be sure to be guided by their advice and example.'[25]

His son, John Stuart Mill, was even more adamant:

'It is so important that the electors should choose as their representatives wiser men than themselves, and should consent to be governed by that superior wisdom . . . that it seems impossible to lay down for the elector any positive rule of duty . . . Individuals, and peoples who are acutely sensible of the value of superior wisdom, are likely to recognise it, where it exists, by other signs than thinking exactly as they do.

To ensure this, the fanchise would have to be weighted in favour of an *élite*, not indeed of money or land, but 'of authenticated superiority of education.'[26]

This is, however, not the only way of minimizing the impact of democracy on parliament. Another is to allow a reasonably long interval between elections. Only in this way, according to J. S. Mill, can a legislator demonstrate that he need not be 'a mere obedient voter and advocate of their opinions, by which he can render himself in the eyes of his constituents a desirable and creditable representative'.[27] Only in this way, wrote James Madison at the time of the constitutional debate in America, can a legislator acquire any expertise. This

'can only be attained, or at least thoroughly attained, by actual experience of the station which requires the use of it. The period of service ought, therefore, to bear some proportion to the extent of practical knowledge requisite to the due performance of the service.'[28]

A third way of stabilizing a democratically elected parliament is to counter-balance it with a second chamber. Such a chamber may take a form that is irrelevant to this discussion: a hereditary House of Lords or (as in Canada) an appointed Senate stand or fall by *not* being democratic. But even an elected second chamber may fulfil a stabilizing purpose if its size, electoral base and term of service differ from those of the lower house. This is what the authors of the *Federalist* had in mind when they proposed a Senate of the kind which was eventually set up in the United States:

'Every new election in the states is found to change one half of the representatives. From this change of men must proceed a change of opinions; and from a change of opinions a change of measures. But a continual change even of good measures is inconsistent with every rule of prudence and every prospect of success ...

Another defect to be supplied by a senate lies in a want of due acquaintance with the objects and principles of legislation. It is not possible that an assembly of men called for the most part from pursuits of a private nature, continued in appointment for a short time ... should, if left wholly to themselves, escape a variety of important errors in the exercise of their legislative trust ...

A good government implies two things: first, fidelity to the object of government, which is the happiness of the people; secondly, a knowledge of the means by which that object can be best attained.'[29]

THE POLITICIAN AS PROFESSIONAL

Madison was not alone in his demand for expertise in politics, and in his apprehension that excessive democracy would bring bad government. Liberals and Conservatives alike, during the nineteenth century, feared the irruption of the masses into politics. They did so because they accepted the arguments and the vocabulary of the Radicals who talked of 'the will of the people' or 'the will of the majority'. Men like Alexis de Tocqueville, J. S. Mill or Matthew Arnold did not like the prospect of having to live under the 'tyranny of the majority' and wished, by constructing appropriate institutions, to avoid this fate. But they agreed with the Radicals in thinking that 'the people' or 'the majority' were real entities with definable qualities; one had to be an ultra-sceptical reactionary to regard such concepts as absurd or nonsensical. Experience since then has shown that these concepts are not very useful in analysing the political process, for reasons to be more fully discussed below.

More immediately relevant are the reasons why the coming of universal suffrage has disappointed many of the hopes of the early democrats, and failed to confirm the worst fears of their Liberal and Conservative contemporaries. 'All professions', wrote Bernard Shaw, 'are conspiracies against the laity'. To the democrat it is essential that justice, the administration, the social services, the making of laws, should be as accessible as possible to the ordinary citizen and should work in his interests. To ensure this, their workings should be supervised by laymen, and many devices, from juries to parent-teacher associations, exist for this purpose. Pre-democratic conventions—the ceremonial of the Law Courts and of Parliament, the often incomprehensible jargon of statutes and white papers, the Establishment in-jokes which pervade the more literate branches of the mass media—are all obstacles to this popular control, but they are not the most serious. Radical democrats made a great mistake when they supposed that the mysteries of government had been invented solely as a plot to keep the people in ignorance. The misapprehension was a widespread one, and even Lenin believed that after the revolution management and administration would be within the grasp of 'any literate person'.[30]

Within six months he was disillusioned,[31] and for a very elementary reason. The more modern a society, the more advanced its economy, the more specialized and sophisticated becomes the business of running it. The possession of any skill gives the possessor power over those who lack it; this is most directly and obviously true when the skill itself is in the use of political power. The observation of this fact led Robert Michels to formulate his 'iron law of oligarchy':

'It is organization which gives birth to the dominion of the elected over the electors, of the mandatories over the mandators, of the delegates over the delegators. *Who says organization, says oligarchy.* By a universally applicable social law, every organ of the collectivity, brought into existence through the need for the division of labour, creates for itself, as soon as it becomes consolidated, interests peculiar to itself. The existence of these special interests involves a necessary conflict with the interests of the collectivity. Nay, more, social strata fulfilling peculiar functions tend to become isolated, to produce organs fitted for the defence of their own peculiar interests. In the long run they tend to undergo transformation into distinct classes... According to this view, the government, or if the phrase be preferred, the state, cannot be anything other than the organization of a minority... The majority is thus permanently incapable of self-government;... always and necessarily there springs from the masses a new organized minority which raises itself to the rank of a governing class. Thus the majority of human beings... must be content to constitute the pedestal of an oligarchy.'[32]

This thesis has been seminal to much of modern political analysis, even if Michels' statement of it is extreme. The empirical evidence is overwhelmingly in favour of the existence of what the Italian sociologist Gaetano Mosca christened 'the political class', though the ease with which one may join that class, or rise within it, varies greatly from one country to another. All the pressures of twentieth-century life operate towards professionalism and expertise. Most British Members of Parliament are 'professional' politicians in the sense that they have decided to make politics their career (and have to decide this at a fairly early age); and in the sense that parliamentary politics has become a full-time occupation. This is deplored by some on the Right, who have a gentlemanly aversion to making a living out of public service, and by some on the Left who see the professional as too remote from the common man whom he is supposed to represent. The current debate on how to make the House of Commons more professional and expert illustrates this cleavage. Especially within the Labour Party there is a tendency for traditional Left-wingers, like Michael Foot and John Mendelson, to oppose greater committee powers, for they see the floor of the House as the one place where indignant public opinion could make an impact on government.*
Nor has any legislature ever accurately reflected the social compo-

---

*The left-right correlation is by no means complete on this subject. Age is also an important factor: younger members on both sides are more 'efficiency minded'.

sition of the electorate. In their social origins and previous occupations legislators differ from party to party and from country to country, but in every party and every country the professional and managerial classes are over-represented at the expense of manual workers. 'Whether one likes it or not', a recent observer has written,

'politics is a middle-class job and the training appropriate for middle-class jobs is also a training for politics. The dice are loaded by the present structure of society as well as by the natural conditions which govern the job of politics in any society'.[33]

Yet the dice are not hopelessly loaded. 'The people may not really govern themselves', Professor V. O. Key has written, 'but they can stir up a deafening commotion if they dislike the way they are governed'.[34] It does not follow that all democracy and all elections are a farce, simply because Members of Parliament are not invariably the direct executors of their constituents' wishes, or because they are able for lengthy periods to act largely as they please. To regard all oligarchies and all élites as *ex hypothesi* incompatible with democracy is to become the prisoner of one's own dogmatic definitions.

WHO REPRESENTS WHOM?

The debate about political representation is old: in the Western world it goes back 2,500 years. Of the major contributions that have been made to it, two at least are not relevant to contemporary Britain. Direct democracy on the Athenian or Swiss model is out, at least on the national level. So is the type of limited, corporate representation which prevailed from the thirteenth to the eighteenth centuries. Universal suffrage has come to stay. Debate has therefore been effectively narrowed to a small, connected range of issues: what are the rôles and mutual relationships of public opinion on the one hand and an élite of political leaders on the other? What are the assumptions about representation and election on which the parliamentary system of a particular country rests?

In Britain these assumptions are twofold. On the one hand Parliament is not the only representative body in this country. There are local councils; and there are any number of organizations to speak on behalf of special interests—trade unions, professional associations, churches, political parties, groups of do-gooders. Many people indeed feel that these subordinate groups are more effective than Parliament in promoting their particular claims. On the other hand Parliament is the only institution representative of the whole nation. This was so even before universal suffrage; eighteenth-century Tories and Whigs agreed that members sat for one national constituency, not a collection of parochial ones. It is even more strongly the case now that every adult citizen has the vote, even if some decline to make use of it.

There is, however, a major difficulty in calling Parliament collectively, or its members individually, *representatives* of the electorate. A representative is clearly under *some* obligation to his elector, has *some* responsibility towards him and acts to *some* extent with his consent. There are, in any system, widely differing notions as to how close these links ought to be; there may even be sharply divergent estimates of how close they actually are. The nature and the strength of the links depend in any system on two important factors. These are (a) the assumptions prevailing in society about morality and conventions in public life—what might be called the 'political culture' of the country concerned; and (b) the relevant political institutions. In some cases the institutions may be specifically fashioned to enable the system to work in a particular way (without necessarily achieving this); in other cases the fact that an institution has been long established and works reasonably well may in turn affect the political habits of the population. A number of basic questions therefore arise before we can know who represents whom in a given state:

How many and how deep are the divisions of interest or ideology among the population?

For how long have they been habituated to parliamentary institutions?

What is the electoral system in force?

How are parliamentary candidates selected?

How many political parties are there and what is their accepted rôle?

How effective are parties in influencing or transmitting public opinion?

How great is the power of pressure groups, and what is their relationship with parties and MPs?

These are the questions that the remaining chapters will examine. Out of them should emerge some idea of how democratic, and how representative, our electoral system manages to be.

REFERENCES

CHAPTER I

1. Aristotle, *Politics* (trans. E. Barker) (Oxford, 1948), p. 128.
2. Neale, Sir J. E. *The Elizabethan House of Commons* (London, 1949), pp. 140-1.
3. Burke, E. 'Thoughts on the Cause of the Present Discontents', *Works*, [Oxford World's Classics] Vol. II, (Oxford, 1906), p. 38.
4. Beer, S. H. *Modern British Politics* (London, 1965), p. 19.
5. Jennings, Sir I. *Party Politics*. Vol. I: *Appeal to the People* (Cambridge, 1960), p. 10
6. Namier, Sir L. B. *The Structure of Politics at the Accession of George III* (2nd edn., London, 1957), pp. 148-9
7. Cf. Priestley, J. *Essay on the First Principles of Government* (1768); Price, R. *Observations on the Nature of Civil Liberty* (1776); Paine, T. *Common Sense* (1776) and *The Rights of Man* (1792).
8. *H.C. Debates*, 3rd Series, Vol. II, 1345-6.
9. Rousseau, J.-J. *The Social Contract*, [Oxford World's Classics] (Oxford, 1947), pp. 269, 271, 372-3.
10. *Ibid.*, p. 373.
11. *Ibid.*, p. 275.
12. Considérant, V. *La Solution ou le Gouvernement Direct du Peuple* (Paris, 1850). Quoted by Michels, R. *Political Parties. A Sociological Study of the Oligarchical Tendencies of Modern Democracy* (intr. S. M. Lipset) (New York, 1962), p. 75.
13. Quoted by Beer, *op. cit.*, p. 42 n.
14. Rousseau, *op. cit.*, p. 331.
15. Aristotle, *op cit.*, p. 197.
16. Beer, *op. cit.*, p. 41.
17. Birch, A. H. *Representative and Responsible Government. An Essay on the British Constitution* (London, 1964), p. 42.
18. *Ibid.*, p. 29.
19. Burke, E. 'Speech to the Electors of Bristol, on his being declared by the Sheriffs, duly elected one of the Representatives in Parliament for that City, on Thursday, the 3rd of November, 1774', *Works*, Vol. II, pp. 164-5.
20. *The Times*, July 20, 1966.
21. Porritt, E. & A. G. *The Unreformed House of Commons. Parliamentary Representation Before 1832* (Cambridge, 1903), Vol. I, p. 122.
22. Neale, Sir J. E., *op. cit.*, endpaper, p. 31.
23. Bagehot, W. *The English Constitution* (intr. R. H. S. Crossman) (London, 1963), p. 247.
24. *Ibid.*, p. 271.
25. Mill, J. *An Essay on Government* (Cambridge, 1937), p. 72.
26. Mill, J. S. *Representative Government* [Everyman Library] (London, 1910), pp. 319, 320.
27. *Ibid.*, p. 313.

28. Hamilton, A., Jay, J. & Madison, J. *The Federalist Papers*, No. 53.
29. *Ibid.*, No. 62.
30. Lenin, V. I. 'Can the Bolsheviks Retain State Power?' (September, 1917), *Selected Works* (Moscow, 1960), Vol. II, pp. 438-9.
31. Lenin, 'The Immediate Tasks of the Soviet Government' (April, 1918), *op. cit.*, Vol. II, pp. 725, 727; 'Left-Wing Communism: An Infantile Disorder' (1920), *op. cit.*, Vol. III, p. 438.
32. Michels, *op. cit.*, pp. 353-4, 365.
33. Blondel, J. *Voters, Parties and Leaders. The Social Fabric of British Politics* (London, 1963), p. 133.
34. Key, V. O., jr., *Politics, Parties and Pressure Groups* (5th edn., New York, 1964), p. 6.

Parties and the Electoral System

In 1832 the British electoral system changed from a historic to a rational basis. The right to vote and, to a lesser extent, the distribution of constituencies were now derived not from tradition but from first principles. All subsequent changes are merely logical extensions of the principles of 1832, as the opponents of that reform had foreseen. This is true despite the fact that the substantive difference between 1833 and 1967 is much greater than that between 1831 and 1833.

ONE MAN, ONE VOTE

Before 1832 the qualification for the vote in the boroughs had been corporative: because it was, in theory, the community that was represented, the franchise could, and did, vary from one community to the next. After 1832 it was individualistic, and all demands for further reform, beginning with those of the Chartists, were for greater concessions in the direction of individualism. With the Second Reform Act of 1867 all householders, and all lodgers paying more than £10 in rent, were enfranchised in the boroughs. The Third Reform Act of 1884 extended the same qualification to the county constituencies. By 1885 58–60% of the adult male population was entitled to vote.[1] Universal male adult suffrage was not achieved until 1918, when women over 30 also gained the right to vote. In 1928 women, like men, became entitled to vote at the age of 21.

A major concession to individualism came with the Ballot Act of 1872. The secret ballot had been consistently demanded by the Radicals, and had almost been included in the 1831 draft of the First Reform Bill.[2] Athough it involved an important principle concerning the freedom of individual choice, its immediate effect outside Ireland should not be exaggerated. The power to intimidate voters was probably declining, at any rate in the towns, and in the counties ingrained habits of deference could not be instantaneously wiped out by statute.

The Ballot Act was also intended to curb the bribery of electors. In this it was less effective. Only the Corrupt and Illegal Practices Act of 1883, which stiffened penalties, limited candidates' expenses and obliged them to appoint an agent, made British elections relatively clean.

It was not until 1948 that the principle of 'one man, one vote' finally triumphed, for until that date some electors had been entitled to cast more than one vote. There were two qualifications entitling a person to plural voting. The first was the possession of business premises in a constituency where the elector was not already resident. In 1918 the minimum rateable value was fixed at £10 for men and £5 for women. The second was the possession of a university degree. James I had in 1603 created separate constituencies for the Universities of Oxford and Cambridge, in which any MA was entitled to vote. In the course of the nineteenth century the same principle was extended to Trinity College, Dublin, the Scottish universities and the newly-founded universities in England and Ireland. In 1948 there were twelve university members.

Both the business and the university vote undoubtedly favoured the Conservative party at the expense of Liberals and Labour, but the extent has probably been exaggerated. Between the wars the number of business electors amounted to between 1 and 1½% of the whole; the number of university electors to about half that.[3] Before 1918 there was no limit to the number of votes a properly qualified person might cast. After 1918 no-one could cast more than one vote in addition to his residential vote. A business elector had to vote in person in a constituency which might be far from his home; university electors could vote by post, but the registers tended to be unreliable. At general elections between 1922 and 1945 the Conservatives probably owed an average of not less than seven and not more than eleven seats to business voters.[4] Of the twelve university seats eight or nine were generally held by Conservatives or Conservative-minded Independents. At no election since 1918 did plural voting decide which party gained a majority. It has been argued that but for the abolition of plural voting the Labour Party might not have gained its overall majority of six in 1950. But it is equally arguable that whatever benefit Labour derived from its 1948 legislation was cancelled by another of its provisions, namely the postal vote.*

Parallel with the demand for 'one man, one vote' was the demand for 'one vote, one value'. That meant in the first place an equalization of constituencies. All that the 1832 redistribution had done was to alter the balance between the agricultural and the industrial interests:

---

*See below, pp. 88–92.

C

there had been no counting of heads. The redistribution which accompanied the Second Reform Act laid down a minimum population for borough representation. All boroughs below 5,000 were disfranchised, those between 5,000 and 10,000 were to have only one member, and the five largest boroughs were to go up from two to three (although, in an attempt to produce some kind of proportional representation, each elector was to have only two votes.) The redistribution of 1885 abolished all boroughs with less than 15,000 inhabitants and reduced all those with less than 50,000 to one member. The counties and most of the larger towns were subdivided into single-member constituencies. Only 24 of the two-member boroughs survived this reorganization and in 1948 the remaining twelve were abolished. The principle that Parliament represented individuals at last triumphed over that of the representation of communities. Even then the principle of equal-sized constituencies was not yet accepted, though the disparities were greatly reduced. In England the largest constituency was now fourteen times the smallest, compared with thirty-five times in 1865.[5]

It was not until the redistribution of 1918 that one can speak of tolerably equal constituencies; not until 1944 that permanent machinery was set up for periodic revision by the creation of Boundary Commissions, and that the number of qualified electors, not the total population, was to determine the size of the constituency. The Commissions were to report every three to seven years, to establish an 'electoral quota' by dividing the total electorate by the number of seats available, and to recommend electorates 'as near the electoral quota as is practicable', while respecting local government boundaries and avoiding inconveniences of size and shape. The Commissioners made their first report in 1948, the second in 1954. But many local councils, party officials and MPs felt that such frequent disruption was more of a nuisance than a benefit, and the interval between redistributions is now not less than ten and not more than fifteen years. New boundaries must therefore be in force by 1969. Certainly the 1954 boundaries are badly out of date. The following examples of extreme growth and shrinkage show how rapidly people are moving their homes:

	1953	1966
	electorates	
Hitchin	58,666	90,840
Manchester Exchange	55,607	26,400
Billericay	53,050	102,198
Birmingham Ladywood	51,719	25,295

There is, however, a second disparity in constituency sizes which is sanctioned by statute. Northern Ireland, which has had its own parliament since 1922, is deliberately under-represented at Westminster; Scotland and Wales are deliberately over-represented. In 1955 the number of electors per MP in the different parts of the United Kingdom were

England	56,347
Wales	50,034
Scotland	47,717
Northern Ireland	72,713

If the seats in Great Britain (i.e. excluding Northern Ireland) had been allocated according to the same quota, England would have had 12 more seats (523 instead of 511), Wales 3 fewer (33 instead of 36) and Scotland 9 fewer (62 instead of 71). In part the over-representation of Scotland and Wales is a concession to national sentiment, but it is also true that it would be difficult to amalgamate the remoter mountain and island constituencies in order to ensure mathematical justice. These anomalies notwithstanding, the regional distribution of constituencies over the last 140 years illuminates the main shifts of population and economic power: [6]

	1831	1885	1918	1955
Northern counties	72	154	171	167
Eastern counties	50	36	27	26
Midlands	101	90	92	107
London and Home Counties	48	99	126	136
South and West	211	77	69	75
Wales and Monmouth	27	34	35	36
Scotland	45	70	71	71
Ireland	99	101	101	12
Universities	5	9	15	—
	658	670	707	630

The magnetic strength of the South-East emerges most clearly, as does the nineteenth-century rise of the North. In this century the stagnation of the North, the boom of the Midlands and the slow recovery of the agricultural South stand out. The share of Scotland, Wales and Ireland (Northern Ireland only, after 1922) has, of course, been artificially frozen.

The Reform of 1832 is significant because it marked the first breach in the traditional doctrine of representation by community and interest and the first major step towards an individualist doctrine. The reforms of 1944 and 1948 are significant because they mark the final steps in this direction. All double voting was abolished, and with it went the last remnants of 'corporative' representation—that of university graduates and proprietors of business premises. Parliament accepted the principle that constituencies should not only made, but kept, equal; in the interests of equality the minuscule constituency of the City of London, which had survived all other redistributions, went. Of its 10,800 electors, three-fifths* were business voters. Its *raison d'être*, apart from sentiment, was therefore the representation of a special interest, and its retention on these grounds had been urged by such corporatively-minded Conservatives as L. S. Amery.[7]

But the reform which gave to British electoral politics its present shape is that of 1883–85. It was then that the right to vote passed from a minority to the majority, that the greatest inequalities among constituencies were eliminated, and corruption all but suppressed. From the 1820's to the 1880's electoral reform was the outstanding political issue; after 1885, the violence of the suffragettes notwithstanding, this was no longer so. A wide suffrage, combined with single-member constituencies, also helped to give the party structure the shape we know today; indeed, to the modern debate about representation and electoral systems party is central.

THE FUNCTION OF THE PARTY

'The ... proposition, that each is the only safe guardian of his own rights and interests [wrote J. S. Mill] is one of those elementary maxims of prudence, which every person, capable of conducting his affairs, implicitly acts upon, wherever he himself is interested.'[8]

That is one half of the Liberal doctrine of representation. The other half is that the MP himself must follow his own conscience, receiving neither instructions nor subsidies from governments, private patrons or parties. As an ideal it was widespread for most of the nineteenth century; as a description of reality it was never very convincing. Nevertheless, it had its uses, and the need to pay lip-service to the principle of disinterestedness led to changes in parliamentary procedure which made it more difficult for members to speak or vote on measures from which they stood to gain personally. Interests could no longer be furthered as informally or crudely as in the eighteenth century, nor opinion so easily controlled. But interest and opinion there continued to be. Nor where they necessarily those of individuals only. Large groups or classes of men might share an interest or opinion and combine to promote it. In other words, interest and opinion were furthered by party. Few political systems, and no parliamentary sys-

*1945 electorate: total 10,830, business 6,608.

tem, can work without party. No-one has yet discovered how to give effect to George Washington's warning, in his Farewell Address, against 'the spirit of party'. But party systems differ widely and they may be differentiated by several criteria: by the internal organization of the parties, by the number of parties in competition, by the long-term relative strengths of these parties and by the functions they perform in the legislature. These criteria cannot be clearly separated from each other; in particular, the function of parties in a given system must depend on the number of competitors.

As regards the number of parties, it is usual to distinguish between single-party, two-party and multi-party system. The single-party system, because it offers no opportunity for competition, is necessarily authoritarian, though it may vary in this respect from Kemal Atatürk's People's Republican party, which monopolized Turkish politics from 1923 to 1946, to the Nazi party. A two-party system is quite consistent with the existence of minor groupings in addition to the two major competitors; indeed in Anglo-Saxon countries, which are normally considered archetypal for the two-party system, such minor parties are universal.* The multi-party system has predominated in continental Europe and in certain extensions of continental political practice— Israel and some Latin American states, for example. A multi-party system may contain a relatively large number of parties, none of which can, by itself, dominate the political scene (Finland, Holland and Switzerland are outstanding examples); or it may resemble the two-party system in having, among its numerous parties, two competitors who stand out above the rest (for example, Ireland, Belgium and the German Federal Republic); or one party may be overwhelmingly stronger than any of the others (for example, Norway, Italy, Israel). As far as the last two types are concerned, Maurice Duverger's distinction between 'major parties' (which are simply larger than 'minor parties') and 'parties with a majority bent' is useful.[9] Though 'major' parties do not necessarily set out to gain absolute majorities over all their rivals, they may from time to time succeed in doing so.**

*Between 1920 and 1964 there have only once been fewer than six candidates in US presidential elections. In Britain the following parties, in addition to the Liberals, have put up more than one candidate since 1959: Communists, Scottish National, Plaid Cymru, Irish Republican, Republican Labour, Independent Labour Party, Socialist Party of Great Britain, New Liberal, British National Party, Union Movement, Radical Alliance.

**Absolute majorities have in recent times been enjoyed by the Swedish Social Democrats (1940–44), the Norwegian Labour Party (1945–61), the Italian Christian Democrats (1948–53), the Belgian Christian-Social Party (1950–54), the Austrian People's Party (1945–49 and since 1965), the West German Christian Democrats (1953–61) and in Ireland by Fianna Fail (1933–43, 1944–48 and 1957–61).

The different types of parties can be more easily understood by looking at their function within the political system. British parties have their origin within Parliament, and became important through Parliament's victory in its struggle for supremacy against the King. Once it was established—as it was in the Revolution of 1688—that Parliament could dispose of the crown, and that no revenue could be raised without its consent, it followed that Parliament possessed a general veto over the monarch's policy. Parliament had begun in the thirteenth century as a consultative body; by the beginning of the eighteenth its members had the power to decide whether they supported or opposed the Administration of the day. Party, however loosely organized, thereby became an instrument of government, and the dividing line between parties was the question of support for the government. That, in essence, is why historically there have been two main parties in British politics. Party allegiance did not have to rest on principle. It could be dictated by personal prejudice, family connection or financial interest. Parties certainly did not require a mass of organized adherents: until the end of the nineteenth century they were what Max Weber would have classified as 'cadre parties' (*Honoratiorenpartei*) as opposed to 'mass parties'. Policy was made *ad hoc* by the parliamentary leaders; candidates, if not nominated by patrons, were self-appointed; constituency organization, in so far as it existed, was in the hands of a few local notables. By the end of the eighteenth century party had developed sufficiently to inspire Burke's definition of it: 'Party is a body of men united, for promoting, by their joint endeavour, the national interest, upon some particular principle in which they are all agreed.'[10] Party is not contrasted here with the national interest, it is equated with it. A party should be able, for a limited period, to take over the running of the state and, for the time being, to be identified with it.

As a description of party in his own day, Burke's words are unrealistic. Some of the odium of faction or conspiracy still hung about the word. Nor did a neat division into 'government' or 'opposition' exist, in the way that Burke's prescription implies, for then a party must either be promoting the national interest in office, or challenging those who are. As long as the monarch was still actively engaged in politics, opposition could entail disloyalty, if not treason and the process of legitimation was a low one. 'The Opposition' as a collective noun began to be used in the 1730's, and the convention that supporters and opponents of the government should sit on different benches facing each other, arose, as far as we can tell, at the same time.[11] It was not until 1826 that the phrase 'His Majesty's Opposition' was first used, and then in a spirit of badinage.[12] It was only after the First Reform Act, when the Crown was deprived of the parliamentary patronage which it had enjoyed through the so-called Treasury boroughs, that a genuinely neutral monarch could be served, in alternation, by one of two competing bodies of men.

The function of a party in a multi-party system differs radically from this. A party of the Anglo-Saxon type is primarily an instrument of self-government, even when the franchise is restricted. Multi-partism presupposes a sharp distinction between party and state. In most continental European states, where there is no long-standing tradition of parliamentarism, but instead one of bureaucratic absolutism, there may even be a sense of the underlying hostility between them. The separation between the 'unofficial' party and the 'official' state is emphasized by the nineteenth-century Swiss jurist Johann Caspar Bluntschli:

'Party is, as the word itself implies, only part of a greater whole, never this whole itself . . . It must never identify itself with this whole, with the people or the state . . .

Parties are not state institutions, . . . not members of the state organism, but free social associations whose formations depend upon a changing membership united for common political action by a definite conviction.'[13]

Benjamin Constant in 1816 defined party in the continental sense even more succinctly: 'A party is a group of men professing the same principle'.[14] What is absent is Burke's reference to the national interest —not because the leaders of continental parties necessarily lack patriotism, but simply because the party is not seen as a suitable instrument for promoting it.

The function of a party in a multi-party system is, quite literally, to 'represent'. The emphasis may be on an ethnic grouping, an economic class, or some philosophical imperative. Where deeply-held religious controversies or long-established ethnic differences cut across each other, or across the recognized economic dividing lines, multi-partism is inescapable. Sometimes the fragmentation of loyalties can be extreme. In the parliament of the multi-national Habsburg Empire there were, on the eve of the First World War, 28 political parties, ranging from Slovene Clericals to Czech Agrarians; in the various successor-states which emerged from the collapse of that Empire only the Communist parties attempted to embrace more than one nationality, religion, class or region. Even within Weimar Germany, which was ethnically homogeneous and administratively fairly centralized, regional and occupational particularism flourished. What is one to make of the Bavarian Farmers' League, The Württemberg Winegrowers' and Farmers' Union—or for that matter the People's Bloc of Inflation Victims or the party of the Vital Interests of Celibates? These are clearly not instruments of self-government. They are, rather, instruments for securing concessions from the state on behalf of a particular interest, or preventing encroachments by the state on the prerogatives of that interest. Because the interest represented is almost always a minority of the social whole, or because it is concerned with speaking only on a limited range of subjects,* government by coalition becomes the norm. Cabinets are constituted not as the direct result of choice by the electors, but as the result of bargaining among the elected.

Since the system is not designed to let a single party take governmental responsibility to the exclusion of all others, and since this party would probably not be trusted to use its monopoly in moderation, coalitions often continue even when one of the parties succeeds in gaining an outright majority. By way of contrast, in an Anglo-Saxon state, minority government is preferred to coalition when no party obtains an absolute majority.**

'Majoritarian' parties, it is evident, serve a different purpose in politics from 'major' or 'minor' ones. Yet, the real problems of government in modern states being what they are, there is some overlap. The Conservative and Labour parties in this country, Republicans and Democrats in the USA to a rather lesser extent, do have definable principles, even if not doctrinaire ideologies, and each of these parties has some supporters who are loyal to it for doctrinaire rather than pragmatic reasons. Similarly, even a non-majoritarian party can hardly ignore the national interest. It is always tempting to persuade others, and not too difficult to persuade oneself, that what is good for oneself is good for one's country; that a prosperous agriculture, or full employment, or Church supervision of schooling, or toleration for Anabaptists, are in the national interest. Moreover, the coalition government, once constituted, cannot restrict itself to debating the ethics of divorce or the validity of historical materialism. Everyday problems of economics, defence and foreign policy cannot be ignored. The election manifesto must contain at least some reference to the party's intentions in these fields beside the recitation of its immutable prin-

---

*Since most people belong to more than one social category, they have some choice in the 'interest party' they can support. In a given state, where the majority of the population are Catholics, the party devoted to the maintenance of Catholic interests may yet remain in a minority, because some Catholics prefer to give priority to the protection of their interests as wage-earners, businessmen, or recipients of fixed pensions.

**e.g. in Britain: 1892–5, 1910–15, 1924, 1929–31; in Canada: 1921–6, 1957–8 and since 1962.

ciples, and its fate at the polls can, after all, depend on its administrative performance.

In this country the history of the Labour Party shows how differing concepts of the rôle of party in our system can co-exist. The Labour Party was intended by its founders to be the representative of a sectional interest whose claims, it was felt, had been ignored by the other parties. Its purpose was defined by Keir Hardie in 1900 as 'promoting legislation in the direct interest of labour', and the 1906 manifesto of the Labour Representation Committee began: 'This election is to decide whether or not Labour is to be fairly represented in Parliament'.[15] The emphasis is clearly on a party of minority status operating on a limited range of issues—not surprisingly, for the example that inspired Hardie and his colleagues was the success of the Irish Nationalist Party under Parnell, equally a sectional party.[16] At the same time it must be obvious that the sectional interest which the party was to represent constituted the majority of the nation, thus permitting the sectional party to become at the same time a majoritarian party. This is in fact what happened, though the process changed the character of the party. But there is no evidence that in the early days any of the party's leaders thought in terms of eventually replacing one of the established groupings in the two-party game.

THE TWO-PARTY GAME

Before a two-party system of the British kind can operate successfully, three conditions need to be fulfilled: historical continuity, social homogeneity and political consensus. To what extent do they exist in Britain, and why?

Historical Continuity. A two-party system can operate most easily when parties originate among politicians within the legislature, rather than among the disfranchised outside it. The notion that it was the function of the legislature to support an Administration in office was —as we have seen—familiar by the end of the seventeenth century. The dichotomy between a 'government' and an 'opposition' party, each ready to assume the running of the country, was familiar by the beginning of the nineteenth century. Indeed, it seems to have been taken for granted that two was the correct number of parties for the proper functioning of a parliamentary system. George W. Cooke, in his *History of Party*, published in 1836, defined his subject as 'the principles and practice of the two classes of statesmen ... which alternately govern a mighty Empire'.[17] The American scholar, A. L. Lowell, was equally certain sixty years later that

'The normal condition of the parliamentary system, . . . among people sufficiently free from prejudices to group themselves naturally, and possessing enough experience to know that the practicable and attainable and not the ideal is the true aim, is a division into two parties, each of which is ready to take office whenever the other loses its majority . . .

A division into two parties is not only the normal result of the parliamentary system, but also an essential condition of its success.'[18]

Lowell later modified his views and it cannot, indeed, be categorically maintained that the triumph of Parliament over the Crown *need* have brought about bi-polarity. But it remains true that the notion of responsibility for government entered into party thinking at an early stage. The idea that 'the King's government must be carried on' and the idea of popular representation in Parliament are therefore not in contradiction to each other, they are complementary. L. S. Amery, who has given us the clearest statement of the Tory view of the constitution in modern times, emphasizes the force of political habit rather than that of political institutions when he says:

'Our whole political life, in fact, turns round the issue of government . . .

The two-party system is a natural concomitant of a political tradition in which government, as such, is the first consideration, and in which the views and preferences of voters or of members of Parliament are continuously limited to the simple alternative of "for" or "against". It is indeed only under the conditions created by such a tradition that there can be any stability in a government dependent from day to day on the support of a majority in Parliament.'[19]

When, therefore, the right to vote was extended in the nineteenth century, the newly enfranchised could accept the idea that they were voting not merely for representatives of their special interests—they were doing that as well, of course,—but also for an administration. Even so, the two-party framework, which had evolved to suit the needs of aristocratic and oligarchic government, might not have survived this transformation if it had been less gradual. Had universal suffrage been grafted on to the British constitution in 1832, it is possible that our party system might not have survived the shock. As it was, none of the Reform Acts up to 1918 was so cataclysmic in its immediate effects that the two existing parties were unable to absorb new divisions of opinion as they arose—industry *versus* agriculture, Church *versus* chapel, democratization *versus* hierarchy, labour *versus* capital.

Gradualness of change is essential for historical continuity, though it cannot by itself guarantee it. But the mass electorate of modern times did not merely inherit parliamentary government; it also inherited a united nation-state and a monarchic dynasty in which the question of succession had long been settled beyond dispute. Any traditional controversies that there might be about the form of the state—monarchy or republic, unitary or federal structure—were dead. London has for centuries been accepted as the capital, in contrast with the metropolitan rivalries of major cities in Germany or Russia. The combination of these factors sufficed to ensure historical continuity, and the historical continuity made it much easier for social homogeneity and political consensus to predominate.

Social Homogeneity. Homogeneity is a relative term, and a subjective one. Much of the recent comment on the British social structure has emphasized the strength of class divisions and class-consciousness, the status-ratings based not merely on occupation, but on region and accent, the inequalities of educational opportunity, and many other aspects all of which would seem to contradict the thesis of homogeneity. But against them must be measured the unifying factors.

Firstly, of the major industrial states, Britain is by far the oldest. This means that we are, and have been for the best part of a century, an overwhelmingly urban nation; more than that, a nation of large city-dwellers. Nearly two-fifths of the population live in the eight major conurbations. Large cities break down regional peculiarities and the differences of character and tradition that flourish in agricultural or sparsely-populated countries: the conditions and preoccupations of life are much the same in Bristol and Bradford. The vast majority of us are employed in industry, or in services indirectly connected with industry: only four per cent. are directly employed in agriculture. Moreover, most farms are large-scale enterprises, making the conditions of work similar to those in industry. Britain lacks a peasant class, and peasants are a powerful force against homogeneity because of their hostility to administrative intrusion, their resentment of industry and city ways and their geographical and cultural isolation, often leading to political separatism.

Secondly, because national unity has been so long established, and because population is so concentrated, regional separatism counts for little. Of course, a Lancastrian or a Cornishman may be proud of his county's attributes; much sentiment and prejudice, as well as some truth, is talked about the differences between North and South, but these differences hardly undermine the sense of national allegiance. In Scotland and Wales national sentiment is stronger and may even be growing, but Scotland and Wales between them amount to only one-sixth of the population of Great Britain, the number of people who speak Welsh or Gaelic is declining and the number who speak no English at all is now negligible.

Thirdly, cultural unity is further strengthened by the absence of notable religious cleavages. In matters of religious observance Britain is a largely indifferent country. In so far as it is not, it is an overwhelmingly Protestant country. Protestants are, it is true, divided into the Church of England on the one hand and the Nonconformist (or Free) Churches on the other—Methodists, Baptists, Congregationalists, Quakers, Presbyterians (though the Presbyterians are, in Scotland, the Established Church). Throughout the eighteenth and nineteenth centuries the differences between Church and chapel were one of the major causes of religious cleavage. These could be vehement: as late as 1902 some Non-conformists went to prison rather than pay rates which would be used to subsidize Anglican schools. But though Nonconformists for long suffered discrimination and contempt they were not, after 1688, persecuted. Religious passions, even at their height, were not as fierce as they tend to be in Catholic countries.

Regional, linguistic and denominational difference all have their effects on political conflict and party allegiance,* but the conflicts take place in a framework of co-existence and are not fought out to the death. There has, it is true, been one major exception to this rule in the last 200 years. In Ireland a Catholic peasant community, with a strong sense of national identity, created a separatist movement and its own sectional political party. Perhaps it was a matter of luck that the Irish dispute was solved without doing more damage to our constitutional framework, and it remains true that the politics of Northern Ireland to this day show a degree of sectarian bitterness generally lacking in Britain. But it is now a fact that British political homogeneity has survived the Irish Question.

Of all the cleavages in British society, by far the most important is that of class. Class-consciousness is the biggest single determinant of both social and political behaviour. Yet this, too, needs to be seen in perspective. In the first place, the British have acquired their reputation for class consciousness in part because it is the *only* major dividing line in British society. We lack the linguistic conflicts of Canada or Belgium, the strong regional peculiarities of the USA or Spain, the Protestant-Catholic divisions of Holland, Germany or Switzerland, the conflicts between supporters and opponents of the Church in countries such as France or Italy, which are, nominally, overwhelmingly Catholic. That leaves only class, with all its rich variations—education, occupation, residence, accent, vocabulary. But precisely because class

*Examined in detail in Chapter IV.

differences are relatively undistracted by religious or ethnic minority problems, because the class conflict is a nation-wide one, class is itself a factor making for national unity. As a result, the major political issues which divide opinion are felt equally strongly throughout the country. What affects voters in Dorset also affects voters in Northumberland. Class could undermine national unity only if conflicts assumed revolutionary intensity, and this has for a long time not been so. True there is a separate working-class 'sub-culture' with its own social customs, values and entertainments, though even it is being slowly undermined by the mass media.[20] But this sub-culture stops short of alienation from the political system. For all the prevalence of 'us/them' dichotomies, most working men do not feel that because they are working men they are second-class citizens and need, for self-protection, to inhabit a separate world. No political movement has tried, like the Social Democratic Party of Germany, or the Communist parties of Italy and France, to envelop their whole social and cultural existence in a self-contained catacomb.

The social homogeneity of Britain is relative: all that can be said of it is that it is greater than in most other countries. It is politically important, because it is essential to the functioning of the two-party system, for without it the necessary political consensus could not exist.

Political Consensus. 'Consensus' is a fashionable and much abused word. It can, for instance, mean widespread agreement on the importance of a particular issue or on a particular policy. It is said that President Johnson tries to achieve a 'national consensus' on US policy in Vietnam, or on such domestic issues as civil rights and the anti-poverty programme. Or that Mr Wilson, in his attempts to impose sanctions on Rhodesia, or in implementing the Prices and Incomes policy, tries to create—or act in accordance with—a consensus. This implies little more than bi-partisanship or supra-partisanship: an attempt to gain support for a particular line of action from those who are normally indifferent to politics, or who normally support the opposing party. It implies also that any dissentient from the consensus policy appears peculiar, idiosyncratic, even suspect. Consensus of this kind need not arise out of a normally conciliatory political atmosphere. Indeed the manufacture of a specific consensus, say over an aggressive foreign policy, may be a device for uniting an otherwise highly fragmented or fissiparous community.

Endemic, as opposed to epidemic, consensus does, however, require a normally conciliatory atmosphere. This is a consensus about 'how' rather than 'what'. Both sides, followers as well as leaders, must be prepared to accept alternation in power, and the legitimacy of the decisions which their opponents make when in office. Most discussion of how strong this consensus is in Britain has tended to be subjective and impressionistic, though the circumstantial evidence that there has been no serious threat of revolution or civil war for more than a century does tempt one to argue from the effect to the cause. There is, however, some recent survey evidence which confirms these impressions. A comparative survey conducted in five countries during 1959–60 revealed the following differences in attitudes to politics:

1. Presented with nine attributes of their nation, respondents were asked which of them they felt proud of. On 'governmental and political institutions' the replies were[21]

	%	Order of preference
USA	85	1
UK	46	1
Germany	7	6
Italy	3	5
Mexico	30	1

2. Asked whether they felt free to discuss politics with others, they replied[22]

	With anyone	With a few	No/Don't know
USA	29	34	37
UK	29	35	36
Germany	23	14	63
Italy	22	15	62
Mexico	19	22	56

3. The proportion of respondents who refused to reveal how they had voted was[23]

	%
USA	2
UK	2
Germany	16
Italy	32
Mexico	1

4. Asked whether they would be displeased if a son or daughter married a supporter of the major opposing political party, they replied in the affirmative.[24]

	Right-wing parent %	Left-wing parent %
USA	4	4
UK	12	3
Germany	19	8
Italy	58	14
Mexico	22	24

Survey evidence also shows that most people in Britain accept the idea that a political party must govern, as well as represent. In 1960, supporters of all parties agreed that the most desirable qualities in a party leader were that he be a 'strong leader' (56%) and 'strong enough to make unwelcome decisions' (47%)[25], both of them attributes of executive leadership. It can, of course, be objected, that we do not know how sincere these answers are. Some people give the answers that they think are expected of them, others repeat official civic values rather than their private (and perhaps selfish or nihilistic) views. This is an objection of limited validity. The fact that people are willing to pay lip-service to official norms of behaviour tells us something about the strength of these norms in the society concerned.

A party which is primarily the expression of an ideology or the representative of a sectarian interest can join in a multi-party coalition, but it is not suitable for a system of two-party alternation. Majoritarian parties must be comprehensive parties. They are not only coalitions of individual interests which left to themselves, could never hope for a share of political power; they are also, to some extent, competitors for the good-will of some of these interests—farmers, owner-occupiers, old-age pensioners and so on. In this sense both the Labour and Conservative parties are comprehensive parties, though both may sometimes stress ideological or sectarian themes for internal party consumption. So is the Liberal party which, whatever its present numerical weakness, nevertheless has majoritarian aspirations. All other parties which contest British elections are, significantly, single-issue or at least single-ideology parties.*

If, as sometimes happens, there is an attempt to turn a comprehensive party into a sectarian or ideological one, this is generally regarded as disastrous for the party concerned. In Britain this applied to the Labour Party in 1960 when, at the Scarborough conference, a motion committing the party to unilateral nuclear disarmament was passed. In the eyes of many, and certainly of those opposed to unilateralism, this turned a party which has survived by virtue of being different things to different people, into a vehicle for pressing an extreme view on a single issue. It happened in the USA in 1964 when Senator Goldwater, an extreme conservative, was adopted as presidential candidate for the Republican Party. One liberal American commentator went so far as to comment

'[Goldwater] has broken the usual rules of political conduct by treating a major party as a 'front' organization ... He has altered the character of the party by committing it firmly to an ideology ... If he

*See above, p. 37.

is successful, whether elected or not, in consolidating this party coup, he will have brought about a realignment of the parties that will put the democratic process in this country into jeopardy...

The achievement of the Democratic party over the past thirty years has been testimony to the effect of the consensual ethos... Naturally the constant task of accommodating broad differences under the same roof has regularly led to the blurring of issues, to a great deal of juggling and about-facing by the skilled professionals. It has also led to a built-in pattern of hypocrisy. But the American political party is based on the understanding that in politics hypocrisy is a minor vice and a major virtue; its other name is tact.'[26]

Above all, both majoritarian parties must be loyal to the parliamentary system, something which is not required of all the contestants under multi-partism. A multi-party system can accommodate a Communist party which regularly polls between 20 and 25% of the total, as in France, Italy or Finland; it could even have accommodated a Nazi party which polled, at the height of its support, 37% of the total, had the remaining parties been agreed on giving priority to the preservation of the Republic. A two-party system clearly cannot accommodate such a party.

'ONE VOTE, ONE VALUE'

The principle of 'one man, one vote' is now part of the electoral law of the land. The critics of our electoral system, however, complain that it does not provide 'one vote, one value'. This is not merely because constituencies continue to be of unequal size, despite the efforts of the Boundary Commissioners, but because the distribution of seats in parliament is not proportionate to the votes cast for the various parties. It is even possible for one major party to get fewer votes than the other, but more seats, as in 1951:

Party	% of votes	No. of seats	% of seats	Votes per seat
Labour	48·8	295	47·3	47,521
Conservative	48·0	321	51·4	42,734
Liberal	2·5	6	1·0	121,759
Others	0·7	2	0·3	99,484

Even when this exceptional anomaly does not occur, it is usual for the minor parties to be under-represented at the expense of the major ones, as in 1959:

	% of votes	No. of seats	% of seats	Votes per seat
Labour	43·8	258	41·0	47,347
Conservative	49·4	365	58·0	37,671
Liberal	5·9	6	1·0	273,085
Other	0·9	—		

Votes, it is clear, do not have equal values. The objections to this are two-fold, but the distinction between them is often blurred. There is, on the one hand, the individualistic argument: it is unfair that a Labour supporter's vote should (as in 1951 or 1959) be worth less than a Conservative supporter's. It is unfair that a Scottish or Welsh elector's vote should be worth more than an Englishman's or Ulsterman's.* It is unfair that a vote cast in Billericay (electorate: 102,000) should be worth less on a quarter of a vote cast in the Western Isles (electorate: 23,000). It is unreasonable that all those who voted for an unsuccessful candidate should be deprived of a representative of their choice. On the other hand there is the argument based on collective representation, on the premise that the legislature should be a 'mirror' of national opinion. According to this view, Liberals, Communists or Scottish Nationalists should sit in the House of Commons in exactly the proportions to which votes are cast for them in the country. This pre-supposes that parties and legislatures exist for purposes which we associate with continental multi-party systems—for the representation of interests rather than the formation of a government.

A 'mirror' parliament of this kind can emerge only under a system of proportional representation. This, in turn, raises the larger question: does the electoral system influence the number and size of parties? Or more specifically: would the adoption of a different electoral system change the face of British politics?

It is often argued that proportional representation leads to multi-partism, and the single-member simple-majority constituency to a two-party system. The experiences of Anglo-Saxon countries on the one hand, and of most continental European states on the other, are cited as proof. Yet the evidence as to causality is far from conclusive. It is more likely that the desire for sectional representation inspires the demand for proportional justice, not that the proportional system causes the proliferation of parties.[27] What the proportional system does do is to discourage a reduction in the number of parties. Where the social structure is stable, the number and relative strengths of the parties remains stable, as the charts illustrating the party histories of Sweden and Switzerland demonstrate (Figure II.1) Where the social structure is unstable, parliamentary chaos may indeed ensue. In Germany in 1930, the year in which Hitler made his first big break-

*See above, p. 35.

D

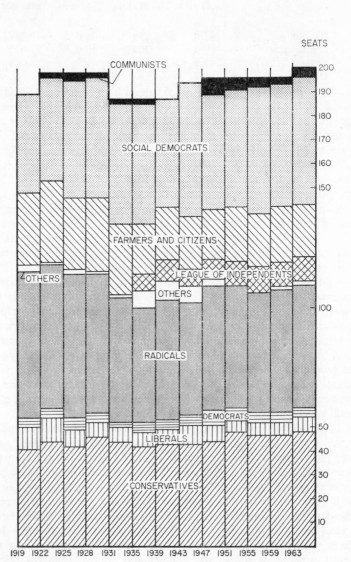

FIGURE II. 1(*a*): Multi-party system in a stable society (*a*) Switzerland

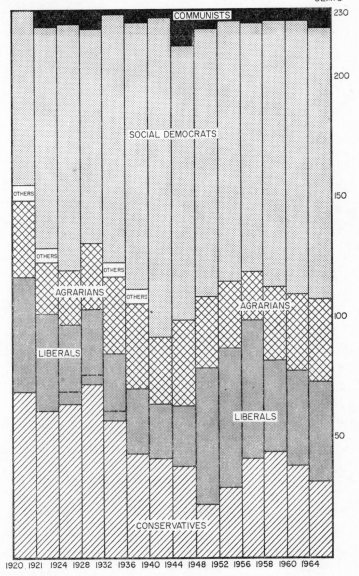

SEATS

COMMUNISTS

SOCIAL DEMOCRATS

OTHERS

OTHERS

OTHERS

AGRARIANS

OTHERS

AGRARIANS

LIBERALS

LIBERALS

CONSERVATIVES

1920 1921 1924 1928 1932 1936 1940 1944 1948 1952 1956 1958 1960 1964

230

200

150

100

50

FIGURE II. 1(*b*) Multi-party in a stable society (*b*) Sweden

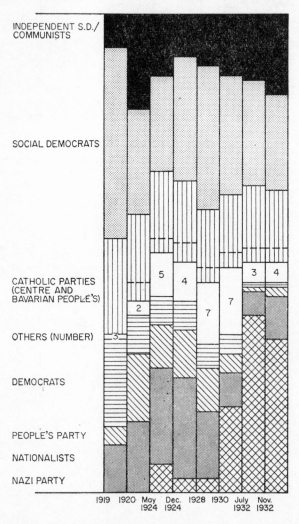

FIGURE II 1(*c*): Multi-Party system in an unstable society: Germany
(in per cent of total vote)

through, no fewer than 35 party groups contested the elections. This fragmentation undoubtedly further weakened the fragile democracy of the Weimar Republic, but it was merely one symptom of the disintegration of German society under the impact of inflation and unemployment. Nothing could be more facile than to suppose that the rise of Hitler could have been halted by the importation of the British electoral system.

That changes in the electoral system may seriously affect the composition of the legislature, without greatly changing the electors' loyalties, is shown by two widely disparate examples, France and Guyana. French multi-partism is often attributed to proportional representation, yet for most of her democratic history France has not operated under this system. From 1875 to 1885, from 1889 to 1919 and from 1928 to 1940 there were single-member constituencies, with a second ballot where no absolute majority had emerged. From 1885 to 1889 there were multi-member constituencies, again with a second ballot where no list had secured an absolute majority. From 1919 to 1927 there was a list system with modified proportionality. Only between 1945 and 1951 was there strict proportional representation by lists. Between 1951 and 1958 lists could combine and obtain all the seats in a constituency if they gained a majority. Under the Fifth Republic since 1958 there have again been single-member constituencies with two ballots.[28] The effect of these changes on voter allegiance and parliamentary strengths may be seen in the example of the Communist Party, which has most to gain from pure proportional representation and most to lose from any system that puts a premium on the ability to form alliances.

French Communist Party. Votes and Seats

	Votes	% of total	No. of seats
1946 (Nov.)	5,431,000	28·2	183
1951	4,934,000	25·9	101
1956	5,427,000	25·6	150
1958	3,870,000*	18·9*	10
1962	3,992,000*	21·8*	41

(votes for metropolitan France only. Figures for 1958* and 1962* relate to first ballot.)

Support for the party, which is based on class-consciousness and ideology, is affected remarkably little by the exigencies of electoral tactics. It lost 82 seats in 1951 because the anti-Communist parties formed alliances; it regained 50 of these in 1956 because the anti-Communists failed to ally. General de Gaulle's electoral appeal deprived it of a quarter of its support in 1958, but his new electoral system deprived it of almost all its seats.

In Guyana (at that time the colony of British Guiana) the British government in 1963 substituted proportional representation for single-member constituencies. The purpose of the exercise was to prevent the People's Progressive Party of Dr Cheddi Jagan from gaining an absolute majority, and in this it was successful. The change in the electoral system made a decisive difference to the composition of the Legislative Assembly, but very little to the number of votes given to the various parties.

Votes and Seats in Guyana

Party	1961 % of votes	Seats	1964 % of votes	Seats
People's Progressive	42·1	20	45·9	24
People's National Congress	41·0	11	40·5	22
United Force	16·3	4	12·4	7
		35		53

Again, there is nothing surprising here. Political loyalties in Guyana are rooted in ethnic community ties and it takes more than a change in rules to shift them.

If the reasons that have been given above for the evolution of the two-party system in Britain are correct—historical continuity, social homogeneity, political consensus—then we do not need the electoral system as an explanation. At the same time, even if it is true that our two parties have evolved for reasons that have nothing to do with the single-member constituency there is no doubt that this system has made it easier for the main parties to maintain their ascendancy. It is the single-member straight-majority system which makes it possible for one or the other party to enjoy a working majority in the House of Commons without necessarily having an absolute majority of the country's votes. Indeed the relationship between votes and seats is almost as predictable in Britain as in countries with proportional representation. Generally speaking, in accordance with the 'cube law'[29] if votes are cast in the proportion of $A:B$, seats are won in the proportion of $A^3:B^3$*.

---

*As a rough guide the cube law has turned out to be valid, provided that both the major parties fight most of the constituencies and there are no gross inequities in constituency boundaries. For exceptions to, and qualifications of, the law, see below pp. 112-3

THE EFFECTS OF PROPORTIONAL REPRESENTATION

Many remedies have been proposed for the injustices of the British electoral system. Only two of them have been seriously discussed. The first is that of the alternative vote. Its purpose is to ensure that within the single-member constituency the elected representative should at least be representative of the majority,* its effect is therefore the same as the second ballot. Instead of marking a cross on the ballot paper against the one candidate he wishes to see elected, the elector marks the candidates 1, 2, 3, (and so on depending on the number of candidates.) If, at the first count, no candidate achieves an absolute majority, the candidate with the lowest number of votes is eliminated and his votes transferred according to the preferences indicated— and so on, until one of the candidates has achieved an absolute majority.

The alternative vote very nearly became law in this country. In 1931 the minority Labour government, which depended on Liberal support, sponsored a bill to introduce it. The bill passed the House of Commons, but the fall of the government ended its career. The alternative vote can undoubtedly give minorities greater influence in that it offers them bargaining power, though it may be objected that this bargaining power goes, in Sir Winston Churchill's words, to 'the most worthless votes given for the most worthless candidates'.[30] It does not, however, give the losing major party greater representation. Calculations of its possible effect in Britain must rest on assumptions about how Liberal voters would have expressed their further preferences. Dr David Butler has calculated that at almost every election since 1918 it would have further exaggerated the majority of the winning party, except in 1950, when it might have led to a Conservative, as opposed to a Labour victory.[31] Even in 1964 it would probably have slightly increased Labour's overall lead of four.[32]

The second important proposal for reform is the single transferable vote, which the House of Commons rejected by only seven votes in

*In 1929 more than half the members (315 out of 615) were elected by a minority of votes, but the number has been as low as 33 (1931) and 37 (1951 and 1955). In 1945 33·4% sufficed to elect the Conservative member for Caithness and Sutherland. Other low winning votes since the war have been:

1962	South Dorset (Labour)	33·5%
1964	Huddersfield West (Labour)	35·8%
1945	Merioneth (Liberal)	35·9%
1945	Orkney & Zetland (Conservative)	36·0%
1946	Caithness & Sutherland (Liberal)	36·1%

In all, eighteen constituencies have been won by candidates polling below 40%, seven of them more than once.

1917. This is a form of proportional representation, based on multi-member constituencies, but does not tie the voter to the list of a single party. Instead, by enabling him to indicate an order of preference for all the candidates, he can, if he wants to, vote for Independents, or candidates of more than one party, as well as discriminating among the candidates of any one party.[33] This system is currently in force in Eire, Malta and in Australia for the Commonwealth Senate. In Britain it was used for electing University members of Parliament between 1918 and 1945, and has been used for electing the House of Laity and the Church Assembly. The Liberal Party advocates 'electoral reform' in its official programme, and this is generally taken to mean STV. They are presumably in favour of it because they hope to benefit from it, while opponents of the change argue that all proportional representation leads to multi-partism and therefore weak government. All discussion must be hypothetical, but there are three main hypotheses which have to be tested:

1. *That the change in the electoral system will have no appreciable effect on people's voting habits.* If this is valid, then the Conservatives would probably still have gained absolute parliamentary majorities in 1955 and 1959, and Labour in 1945. Calculation for the other post-war elections must involve some guess-work. A certain amount depends on how the multi-member constituencies are drawn up, and some allowance must be made for the fact that the Liberals would probably fight more seats. Two different estimates for the 1966 election are

Estimated Party Strengths in 1966
under Single-Transferable Vote

		(1)		(2)
	% of vote	Seats	% of total	Seats	% of total
Labour	47·9	320	50·8	328	52·0
Conservative	41·9	265	42·0	265	42·0
Liberal	8·5	39	6·2	33	5·3
Other	1·7	6	1·0	4	0·7

(1) Estimated by M. Steed, in D. E. Butler & A. S. King, *The British General Election* of 1966, p. 293.
(2) Estimated in *Representation* No. 23, April, 1966, p. 4.

This, however, is the least plausible of the three hypotheses. It is much more likely that a change in the electoral system will lead to some change in voting habits.

2. *That the change in the electoral system will benefit the smaller parties.* This supposes that electors are at the moment deterred from

supporting the party of their first choice by the assumption that its candidate stands no chance of success. A good deal of electoral propaganda is based on the validity of this assumption. In 1964 and 1966 Liberal posters bore the slogan 'If you think like a Liberal, vote like a Liberal'; in 1950 a Conservative poster (showing a torn ballot paper) read, 'A vote for the Liberal is a vote wasted'. In both 1950 and 1962 the Gallup Poll asked electors whether they would vote Liberal if they thought the Liberals could win. In 1950 34% said 'yes', compared with 9% who actually did; in 1962, just after the Orpington success, 46% said 'yes'.[34] The trouble is that this question refers to an extremely hypothetical situation. It assumes a situation in which the Liberal Party *nationally* is a challenger for power (as it last was in 1929), rather than to one in which the Liberal was *locally* in a winning position. Before this could happen there would have to be a major re-alignment of party forces, brought about by other factors than electoral reform. One can only say that if the change to proportional representation encouraged voting for minor parties, then absolute majorities in the House of Commons would indeed become the exception rather than the rule. Whether Britain would, as a result, be worse governed, is an altogether different question; the advocates of STV are bound to argue that it would not.[35]

3. *That the change in electoral system will be detrimental to the smaller parties.* This seems, on the face of it, contrary to all accepted ideas. Yet, if it is true that people in this country vote for a government rather than primarily for the representation of an ideology or an interest, then parties capable of forming a government single-handedly will be even better off under STV. At present the major parties gain from the 'wasted vote' argument in marginal seats, but lose by it in safe seats. For in a safe Conservative seat it is the Labour votes that are principally wasted, and there is a strong incentive to cast them instead for a minor party with a wider local appeal—Liberal, Welsh Party or Scottish Nationalist. In the constituencies where Liberals increased their share of the poll between 1959 and 1964, they did so principally at the expense of the minority party.[36] The twelve seats which the Liberals have gained at by-elections or general elections since 1958 include only one which could also have been gained by the other major party (viz. Caithness & Sutherland); the other eleven were all, from a two-party point of view, safe seats*. Of the eleven other seats in which the Liberals have, since 1959, come to within

*Torrington (1958), N. Devon (1959), Orpington (1962), Bodmin, Inverness, Ross & Cromarty (1964), Roxburgh, Selkirk & Peebles (1965), Cheadle, N. Cornwall, Aberdeenshire West, Colne Valley (1966).

10% of the winning candidate, only three are marginal.* The general
rise in support for the Liberal Party since the early 1950's has been
almost entirely restricted to safe seats. Between 1950 and 1966 there
was a rise of 4.1% in the Liberal vote in safe seats and a decline of
0.3% in marginals. Comparing Liberal performances in the two types
of seat Mr Michael Steed concludes that 'nearly a third of the Liberal
vote can be squeezed into voting for another party'.[37]

But what happens under STV, when every seat is a marginal one?
For those who want the maximum representation of minority views,
no vote will be wasted. For those essentially involved in a plebiscite
between ministerial teams, every minority vote will be wasted.

THE FUTURE OF THE PARTIES

It is easy to exaggerate the continuity and consistency with which
a two-party system has operated in this country. Even in the nineteenth and twentieth centuries the two-party pattern has periodically
broken up—1846-66, 1885-95, 1918-31—only to re-appear in a new
form. The reason for this resilience is that politicians and voters alike
see party not only as the representative of sectional interests and beliefs, but also as an instrument of government. Both politicians and
voters believe, rightly or wrongly, that this task of government is best
entrusted to a single party with an absolute parliamentary majority.
These beliefs prevail because of the way in which the British constitution has developed. They are not the consequence of the simple-
majority system of election, nor of single-member constituencies,
which did not become general until 1885. What is true is that this
method of electing members of parliament exaggerates the gap between the parties, and thus makes single-party government possible. If
it is the exigencies of government and the firmness of traditional loyalties that determine the number of parties, there is no reason to suppose that this country will depart from the pattern of major party
alternation in the foreseeable future. Even a change in the electoral
system need not bring about a major revision—indeed, as we have seen,
it could possibly strengthen the hold that the major parties have.
What can change, of course, and what has changed after every one of
the re-alignments in the past, is the names, composition and aims of
the contestants. It is one thing to forecast, for the long term, a con-
tinuance of two-party competition, quite another to assume that the
parties themselves are therefore immune from major change.

*Safe Con.: Banff, Blackpool N., Chippenham, W. Derbyshire, Tiverton,
Worcester. Safe Lab.: Paisley, Merioneth. Marginal: High Peak, Leicester N-E,
Rochdale. Seats previously held by Liberals, but lost by less than 10%, are
excluded.

REFERENCES

CHAPTER II

1. Blewett, N. 'The Franchise in the United Kingdom, 1885-1939', *Past and Present* 32 (December, 1965), p. 30.
2. Butler, J. R. M. *The Passing of the Great Reform Bill* (London, 1914), p. 180.
3. Butler, D. E. *The Electoral System in Britain since 1918* (Oxford, 1963), p. 147.
4. *Ibid.*, p. 148.
5. *Whitaker's Almanack*, 1875, pp. 90-2; *ibid.*, 1885, pp. 121-9.
6. Taken from Jennings, Sir I., *Party Politics*, Vol. I, *Appeal to the People*, pp. 26, 31, 37
7. Quoted by Butler, D. E., *op. cit.*, p. 73.
8. Mill, J. S. *Representative Government*, p. 208.
9. Duverger, M. *Political Parties* (London, 1954), p. 283.
10. Burke, E. 'Thoughts on the Cause of the Present Discontents', *Works*, Vol. II, p. 82.
11. Foord, A. S. *His Majesty's Opposition* (Oxford, 1964), pp. 155-8.
12. *Ibid.*, p. 1.
13. Bluntschli, J. C. *Lehre vom Modernen Staat* (Stuttgart 1875-6), pp. 499, 504. Quoted by H. Arendt, *The Origins of Totalitarianism* (2nd edn., London, 1958), pp. 253-5.
14. Duverger, *op. cit.*, p. xiv.
15. Bealey, F. & Pelling, H. *Labour and Politics, 1900-1906. A History of the Labour Representation Committee* (London, 1958), pp. 28, 264.
16. Pelling, H. *The Origins of the Labour Party* (2nd edn., Oxford, 1965), p. 55.
17. Cooke, G. W. *The History of Party. From the Rise of the Whig and Tory Factions in the Reign of Charles II to the Passing of the Reform Bill* (London, 1836-7), pv.
18. Lowell, A. L. *Governments and Parties in Continental Europe* (Boston-New York, 1896), Vol. I, pp. 71-2.
19. Amery, L. S. *Thoughts on the Constitution* (Oxford, 1947), pp. 16-7.
20. Cf. Hoggart, R. *The Uses of Literacy* (London, 1957); Jackson, B. & Marsden, D. *Education and the Working Class* (London, 1962); Runciman, W. G. *Relative Deprivation and Social Justice. A Study of Attitudes to Social Inequality in Twentieth-Century England* (London, 1966).
21. Almond, G. A. & Verba, S. *The Civic Culture. Political Attitudes and Democracy in Five Nations* (Abridged edn., Boston-Toronto, 1965), p. 64.
22. *Ibid.*, p. 82.
23. *Ibid.*, p. 80.
24. *Ibid.*, p. 97.
25. Abrams, M., Rose, R. & Hinden, R. *Must Labour Lose?* (London, 1960), p. 25.

26. Hofstadter, R. 'Goldwater and his Party', *Encounter* 133 (October, 1964), pp. 2, 3-4.
27. For the argument that proportional representation causes multi-partism, see Duverger, *Political Parties,* pp. 216-55; Schattschneider, E. E. *Party Government* (New York, 1942), pp. 64-85; Hermens, F. A. *Democracy or Anarchy? A Study of Proportional Representation* (Notre Dame, 1941), passim.
28. Campbell, P. W. *French Electoral Systems and Elections since 1789* (2nd edn., London, 1965), pp. 71, 75-6, 79-80, 90-5, 97-8, 103-5, 113-4, 128-30.
29. Kendall, M. G. & Stuart, A. 'The Law of Cubic Proportions in Election Results', *British Journal of Sociology* I (September, 1950); Butler, D. E., *op. cit.,* p. 195.
30. Quoted by Lakeman, E. & Lambert, J. D. *Voting in Democracies. A Study of Majority and Proportional Electoral Systems* (London, 1955), p. 64.
31. Butler, *op. cit.,* pp. 192-4.
32. Steed, M. 'Alternative Vote and the Speaker's Conference', *New Outlook* 49 (November, 1965), p. 11.
33. For a lucid exposition of how STV works, see Lakeman & Lambert, *op cit.,* pp. 98-131.
34. *Gallup Political Index,* September, 1962, p. 164
35. *Ibid.,* pp. 227-33.
36. Berrington, H. B. 'The General Election of 1964', *Journal of the Royal Statistical Society,* Series A, CXXVIII (1965), pp. 42-5.
37. Butler, D. E. & King, A. S. *The British General Election of 1966* (London, 1966), p. 285.

Members and Parties

POLITICAL parties, once they are established as part of the mechanism of parliamentary government, serve two main purposes. On the one hand they are a means of mobilizing electoral support for the measures being debated by the 'political class'; on the other, they are a means by which popular demands and popular grievances can be translated into official policy. The two purposes are conplementary, though they can involve serious clashes of interest.

THE EVOLUTION OF CONSTITUENCY ORGANIZATION

Before 1832, party bonds rested on individual links between notables. Elections took place once every seven years; contests were few*; voters were easily bribed. As for autonomous associations by groups of citizens of the kind that became common towards the end of the eighteenth century—for instance, the Society for Supporting the Bill of Rights (1769), the Yorkshire Association (1779) or the Society of the Friends of the People (1792)—these were clearly suspect as subversive.

After 1832 electoral organization demanded some extension of party machinery. Only in 1918 was the duty of drawing up registers of electors handed to local authorities: until then the biggest task of election managers and agents was to ensure that eligible electors were registered. The Tories set about centralizing the task of registration through the Carlton Club founded in 1832. The Radicals followed suit in 1836 with the Reform Club.[1] But the habits of electioneering were not changed overnight by the Reform Act and contests remained the exception, not the rule. In 1835 there were contests in only 174 out of 401 constituencies.[2] As late as 1868 there were unopposed returns in

---

*In 1761 there were 48, in 1780, 80 (Sir L. Namier, *The Structure of Politics at the Accession of George III*, p. 159; I. R. Christie, *The End of North's Ministry, 1780-2*, pp. 54–57).

210 out of 487 constituencies, in 1880, 110 (145 and 93 respectively if one excludes Ireland).[3] Nor were the parties in Parliament any more coherent. Not until 1867 did the party in power issue whips for the majority of divisions in the House of Commons; not until after 1918 was this usual for the opposition party.[4] Professor Beer's 'coefficient of cohesion' shows that modern party discipline certainly did not exist before 1867 and cannot really be dated earlier than the 1880's.[5] Voluntary associations flourished more easily than before 1832, led by the Chartists (1838) and the Anti-Corn Law League (1839). Groups like these tried to put pressure on parliament through their voting power, as well as by petitions and demonstrations. But, large or small, they were, unlike the parties, devoted to the achievement of a single objective and they steered clear of direct links with the established parties. Mass membership of parties, as opposed to agitational groups, was unknown.

What changed the nature of party organization both inside and outside parliament was the reform of 1867. There were now over two million electors, and no constituencies with fewer than 5,000 inhabitants. Informality in politics was no longer possible. The impetus to further organization came from both above and below. The established party leaders found it more necessary to mobilize opinion, not merely with machines but with policies. To the newly enfranchised it was obvious that the vote should be used to remedy their grievances.

Not surprisingly, the Conservatives were more successful in organizing from above, the Liberals from below; nor is it surprising that the Conservatives were once more first off the mark. The interests which the Conservatives existed to defend—land, aristocracy, Church, monarchy—formed a more coherent amalgam than the uneasy 'Liberal' coalition of Whigs, capitalists and Radicals, and they were more seriously threatened by the advance of democracy. Moreover, the Conservatives had a more self-confident and clear-cut view of the proper relation between leaders and followers. Working-men were to be invited to confide in the natural leaders of society, but not to dictate to them. The National Union of Conservative and Constitutional Associations, which evolved between 1867 and 1885 under the lead of John E. Gorst and Lord Randolph Churchill, was intended to be a 'handmaiden'.[6] Except during the brief period of Lord Randolph Churchill's ascendancy (1883–86) it has never claimed to be a policy-making body, though its views could not always be ignored. Until 1965 the party's leader graced its annual conference only on the final day. 'Tory Democracy' as Lord Randolph christened his policy, referred to the relationship between the new mass electorate and the traditional party leadership, not primarily to a policy of social reform, though it followed that some programmatic attractions were needed to ensure the loyalty of the masses.

The Liberals were in a more difficult position. Like the Whigs after 1832, they were divided into those who desired no further reform and agreed with the Tories on the need to protect parliament from mob control, and those Radicals for whom the final political objective was the subordination of the representative to the voter. To establish constituency organizations was therefore to risk playing into the hands of the Radicals. This is indeed what happened. Constituency organization arose naturally enough through the need to mobilize Liberal supporters in the large cities. This was especially urgent in three-member boroughs where each elector had only two votes* and where Liberal votes had to be evenly spread among the three candidates to ensure a clean sweep. This is what the Birmingham 'caucus' under Joseph Chamberlain and Francis Schnadhorst first achieved. But the large cities were also the strongholds of Radicalism. The purpose of the National Liberal Federation, which was founded in 1877 under the auspices of the caucus, was not merely to extend organizational efficiency; it was, according to Chamberlain, 'that the people at large should be taken into the counsels of the party'. The invitation to the first conference stressed 'the direct participation of all members of the party in the formation and direction of policy'.[7] Even in the Liberal Party the Federation never formally gained the constitutional right to make policy, although its influence, especially in the 1880's and 1890's, was much greater than that ever achieved by the National Union.

The Labour Party, entirely a product of the age of mass participation in politics, had indeed constituency organizations long before it became, in the conventional sense, a national party. The Labour Representation Committee, as it was known from 1900 to 1906, was a confederate body to which trade unions and socialist societies belonged collectively. By 1906 there were a hundred local LRCs with the responsibility of nominating candidates;[8] elsewhere the task rested on the Trades Council, a body in which the local trade union branches came together. As the purpose of the Labour Representation Committees was to challenge the established duopoly of Conservatives and Liberals, constituency organization was the first need. It was only in 1918 that Labour turned itself into a national political party, with local party branches to which individuals, not merely members of affiliated societies, could belong. When it came to deciding the relationship between the rank-and-file and the parliamentary party, Labour's kinship with Radicalism became obvious. Labour was committed to the representation of a particular interest and, after the adoption of a Socialist programme in 1918, a particular policy. Labour

* See above, p. 34

MPs were consequently delegates on behalf of a class and a doctrine, not parliamentarians in the eighteenth-century style. Unlike the Conservatives and Liberals, Labour had no tradition of leadership by social superiors, and the whole temperament of Labour supporters was hostile to the idea that their leaders, once elected, could know better than their followers where their true interests lay. Independence could only be an excuse for betrayal. This is the origin of the unhappy conflict for supremacy between the party conference and the parliamentary party which has bedevilled Labour's history.*

In the mid-twentieth century the constituency party is an integral part of the national party organization. Disputes arise from time to time concerning individual branches and there are no doubt the normal tensions that exist between generals and officers in the field. *De facto* the constituency branches of all three parties are handmaidens, though they are handmaidens enjoying a good deal of autonomy and discretion. Their main duties are to nominate parliamentary candidates, to collect money, to canvass supporters and get them to the poll, and to distribute propaganda in support of the party's policy. The whole of their activity is therefore dominated by elections, whether parliamentary or municipal; and municipal elections, however importantly they may loom to local functionaries, are seen by headquarters in London as a way of lubricating the general election machinery.

SELECTING THE CANDIDATE

'Adoption is hell for the candidate, pure joy for those that select him. The choice of a candidate is for the constituency party worker the reward of many years of hard, unglamorous work. It is a pleasure to be savoured. Whereas he would normally 'look up to' his candidate, and will tend if not to praise at least to justify him, it is at the selection conference that he comes briefly into his own. Then it is "they" who are the suppliants, he who calls the tune.'

These are the words of a former Conservative MP in an article rather ungraciously entitled, '*Government by Greengrocer*'.[9] They apply with equal force to the Labour Party. With one major qualification, local parties are free to hire and fire as they choose, even if the freedom of choice is in practice often limited.

That party headquarters should be involved in the selection process at all is a symptom of the move from oligarchical to mass politics. Approval by the leadership became a condition in the Conservative Party in 1874.[10] The present machinery dates from 1935 when the

*See below, pp. 139-41.

Standing Advisory Committee on Candidates (SACC) was set up
Apart from specifying selection procedure, SACC draws up the 'List of
Approved Candidates', which local associations are urged, but not
required, to consult and it has a power of veto over anyone selected.[11]
Only one major change has been made since then. Up to 1948 it was
open to any candidate or MP to offer to pay his own election expenses
and to make general annual subscriptions. This had the obvious consequence of making it easy for rich men to buy good seats and of barr-
ing poor, talented aspirants. But it had the additional disadvantage of
branding the Conservatives as the rich man's party, and of weakening
the organization where it did not have to bother with fund-raising.
Since 1949 constituency associations have had to meet all election
expenses out of member's subscriptions. Donations are limited to
£25 per year for candidates and £50 per year for MPs, and must not
be made a condition of selection.[12]

The Labour Party, because of its loose organization, was in no
position to impose control over candidates before 1918. All that had
been required was a signed pledge to accept the constitution of the
party, to obey the decisions of the parliamentary party, and to abstain
from campaigning under different party labels or in opposition to other
Labour candidates.[13] Even this was dropped in 1911 when doubts
arose as to its legality. The present 'Model Rules' date in their essence
from 1929–30. Transport House, the party headquarters, maintains two
lists of candidates: List A contains the names of those who have been
sponsored by a trade union affiliated to the party and approved by the
National Executive Committee (NEC) of the party. List B contains the
names of other individuals who wish to be considered. As in the Conservative Party, a Constituency Labour Party (CLP) is not required
to consult either list, but individuals cannot simply present themselves. They need to be nominated by a body affiliated to the CLP, such
as a trade union, a ward committee or a co-operative society. Selection
is also subject to approval by the NEC; again, as in the Conservative
Party, inclusion in List B is not in itself a guarantee of this. In
its financial arrangements the Labour Party has fewer safeguards
against dependence on patrons than the Conservatives. Though individuals are now limited to donating £50 a year, a union sponsoring a
candidate may (but by no means always does) contribute generously
within the maxima laid down in 1957.[14] Between 1945 and 1959
some 220 constituencies received grants from unions and 45 from the
Co-operative movement.[15]

What do the residual central powers amount to? Nether party headquarters wants to buy trouble. The leaders of both parties know that
they lead heterogeneous coalitions of sometimes highly sensitive groupings on whom, in the last resort, the coherence of the party's organiza-

E

tion depends. All public quarrels are bad publicity. Action is therefore taken only when inaction is the greater evil.

Since the war only one Conservative candidate has been disavowed by the SACC—Mr Andrew Fountaine, candidate for Chorley in 1950, who had made an anti-Semitic speech at a party conference and has since become president of the racialist British National Party. Only one constituency association has been disaffiliated. No member of Parliament has been expelled from the party, which would have disqualified him from re-adoption, none has been even deprived of the party whip, though some have voluntarily resigned it. In 1959 Sir David Robertson, MP for Caithness & Sutherland, who had resigned the Conservative whip retained the *de facto* support of his association. Neither he nor Mr Fountaine was opposed by an 'official' London-sponsored candidate.

The Labour Party has greater ideological difficulties and needs to guard against infiltration from the far Left as well as deviation towards the Right. In the 1945–50 parliament five MPs (four on the Left, one on the Right) were expelled from the party, of whom one (Mr Konni Zilliacus) worked his passage back. The various MPs who have lost the parliamentary whip, were all re-admitted in time for the subsequent general election. The NEC has since the war withheld approval from five candidates adopted by constituencies, four of them left-wingers. Two of them have subsequently re-appeared as (unsuccessful) candidates in other constituencies. What is not known is how many names have been kept off the B List. Before 1960 scrutiny of the list was very lax.

The almost automatic right of a sitting member to re-adoption has long been an axiom of British politics. Yet constituencies do from time to time try to unseat their incumbents, generally for personal failings—neglect of duties, old age, possibly drunkenness or a lapse from sexual decorum. Professor Ranney has calculated that between 1945 and 1964 known attempts to enforce retirement totalled eighteen for the Conservatives and sixteen for Labour. In each party twelve of the attempts were successful.[16] Here, too, the constituencies meet little resistance from party headquarters unless there are obviously procedural irregularities or blatant challenges to the authority of the national leadership. Thus Transport House has twice successfully resisted the attempts of left-wing CLPs to get rid of MPs who were judged too 'loyal' to the leadership.*

On the face of it, these powers of selection and rejection would seem to make local party branches anything other than 'handmaidens'.

---

*Mrs Bessie Braddock (Liverpool Exchange) and Miss Elaine Burton (Coventry South), both in 1955. (Ranney, *op cit.*, pp. 188–91.)

After all, if Harold Wilson or Edward Heath had failed to convince their constituency selection committees they might today not be leading their parties. The real situation is rather less melodramatic. Most constituency parties rely on party headquarters to supply them with aspirants. Even if the final choice is made locally, the supply of suitable nominees can, to some extent, be rigged. A person who is both able and ambitious can count on being selected sooner or later; so can anyone whose party is determined to see him in Parliament. At by-elections, as opposed to general elections, both party headquarters take greater care over selection procedure—indeed the Labour Party has special powers to do so—partly because an isolated by-election attracts more publicity than any one single contest in a general election, partly also because front-benchers defeated at the preceding general election may be looking for a way back. But since previous parliamentary experience is one of the qualities a selection committee values most highly, few prominent party members need be in the wilderness for long. Indeed, upward mobility, whereby long-serving members graduate from marginal to safe seats, is a familiar feature of both parties.

'He who can make nominations is the owner of the party' wrote one American scholar.[17] But the centralization of the British system of government and of British political sentiment has led to a degree of party cohesiveness which makes localism count for much less in British than in American Government. Local parties acquiesce in tactful central leadership not out of self-sacrifice but because they are in fundamental agreement with the leadership about the national rôle of the party. There is only one respect in which they exercise a moulding influence: they do, to a considerable extent, determine the social composition of the parliamentary parties.

IS THERE A POLITICAL CLASS?

Whatever else members of Parliament may be representative of, it is not the social composition of their constituents, nor even the social composition of their own voting supporters. We have already noted that this is common form in parliamentary democracies,* and the reasons for this. The professionalism of politics means that it attracts predominantly upper and middle-class people, those who have enjoyed higher education and have managerial or administrative experience. It attracts, in particular, members of the 'talking' and 'communicating' professions—lawyers, teachers, journalists, advertisers. But in addition

*See above, pp. 27-8. There is a useful comparison of the social composition of various legislatures in the *International Social Science Journal*, Vol. XIII, No. 4 (1961).

FIGURE III. I : Background of MPS 1951 and 1966 by (*a*) Occupation
(*b*) Education (in per cent)

to that, a country's political system inevitably reflects its social values and class attitudes: it is not surprising that those who find their way into Parliament have those attributes—whether of education or of occupation—which also make them leaders of society in other respects. A comparison of the backgrounds of Labour and Conservative MPs in 1951 and 1966 shows that there have not been any startling changes. Those that have taken place are towards greater similarity between the major parties and further sway from social representativeness.

Education, which in Britain designates both skill and status, is perhaps the best single criterion for judging how far the two major parties differ from each other, and how far from the population at large. In both parties educational standards have been rising, and this is reflected in the increasing share of the professions—among Conservatives at the expense of businessmen, among Labour at the expense of workers. This has had the paradoxical result of increasing the public school element in the Conservative party as the following table shows: [19]

Educational Background of Conservative
M.P.s, 1945–66

Year	All public schools	%	Eton only	%	Harrow only	%
1945	142	66	57	27	13	6
1951	240	75	76	24	23	7
1955	260	76	78	23	20	6
1959	263	72	73	20	20	5½
1964	229	76	68	22	17	5½
1966	216	85	54	22	14	5½

The relative recovery by Etonians since 1959 does not arise out of an increase in Etonian candidatures; it illustrates that Etonians sit for safer seats, just as public-school men get better seats than men from state schools, even if they are graduates.*

Even among university graduates, who have been gaining in both parties, clear differences remain. Compared with the Conservatives, Labour is distinctly a red-brick party. Conservative graduates of Oxford and Cambridge have consistently been adopted for winnable seats, while those of other universities have not. In the Labour Party the difference is negligible, though in absolute terms red-brick outnumbers 'Oxbridge'. [20]

*1966 figures: Public school, successful 204, unsuccessful 205
State school, successful 49, unsuccessful 103
(Butler & King, *The British General Election of 1966*, p. 208.)

Success of University-educated Candidates, 1950–66

		Conservative		Labour	
			%		%
1950	'Oxbridge'	156	75	55	56
	Other	29	27	74	48
1955	'Oxbridge'	182	72	46	49
	Other	36	40	65	39
1959	'Oxbridge'	181	69	46	43
	Other	35	40	55	40
1964	'Oxbridge'	155	61	60	49
	Other	33	32	74	47
1966	'Oxbridge'	144	54	83	59
	Other	26	27	103	54

The influx of graduates and professional men into the Labour benches has been the biggest single change in the social composition of Parliament since the decline of the aristocratic element in the nineteenth century. It has taken place almost entirely since 1964 and its impact has been even more sudden than a comparison with 1951 would suggest. Of the 72 Labour MPs who have entered parliament since 1964 57% belong to the professions, compared with 41% of those elected in 1964; 68% are university graduates compared with 42% for their predecessors; 14% are workers compared with 32%. In terms of formal education and professional expertise the 1966 parliament is the most highly qualified ever.[21]

It is their continuing predilection for a public-school business or professional man, preferably Church of England, that Conservative constituency associations maintain their most successful and significant defiance of Central Office wishes. Conservative selectors are least prone to change in the county constituencies. Local connections are less necessary than is generally thought;[22] what is important is a promise to live in the constituency after selection*. Even more important is, that the aspirant should be a 'gentleman'.

'The first "player" to be adopted for a county seat [according to Julian Critchley] was Mr John Biffen** ... a village schoolboy who got to Cambridge, he defeated, having been a National Service lance-corporal, a colonel and two majors to win the nomination.[23]

*Mr Christopher Soames, a Conservative ex-Cabinet minister who lost his seat in 1966, declined an invitation to be short-listed for a by-election in Honiton (Devon) on the grounds that he was not prepared to 'uproot his family'.   (*The Times*, January 12, 1967)

**At a by-election in 1961. But Mr Critchley forgot about Mr Ray Mawby, an electrician who has sat for Totnes since 1955.

Central Office urges selection committees to adopt more trade union-ists, more women, more Jews and Catholics and the party conference endorses these views in principle. Yet, if anything, the chances of these 'minority' groups have been declining in recent years. In 1951 there were 23 women candidates, in 1959, 27 and in 1966, 21. In 1951 there were 15 workers, in 1959, 13 and in 1966, 6.[24] This decline is paralleled in the Labour Party where, however, it seems to cause less distress. Catholics, on balance do equally well in both parties. Non-conformists are more numerous and more successful on the Left, as they have traditionally been.[25] Jews find it difficult to get adopted by the Conservative Party and even more difficult to get adopted in winn-able seats. The 1964 parliament saw the largest post-war contingent of Jewish Conservatives in the House—and all three were baronets. In this respect the party has become more exclusive since the beginning of the century. In 1900, out of 12 Jewish MPs, 8 were Conservatives.[26] Do the local parties know their job better than Central Office in this respect? The answer is that they are trying to do different jobs. Pre-sumably nobody in Central Office imagines that the tide could be turned in the crucial marginals by adopting Jewish lady shop stewards instead of retired colonial administrators. What they are concerned with is a *nationally* balanced ticket which will rid the party of the stigma of exclusiveness and privilege.

Within the Labour Party the problem of social balance is the re-verse. Nothing was more natural in the party's early days than that the great majority of its candidates should be working-class and union-sponsored. It did not follow, however, that this was the ideal arrange-ment once Labour became a national party with aspirations to form-ing a government. Though Labour has always had a number of aristo-cratic and intellectual sympathizers, the predominantly 'cloth cap' image was considered a deterrent to recruiting followers outside the traditionally militant industries. A further trouble was that MPs who entered Parliament through union sponsorship were not always of very high calibre, mainly because unions needed their most talented officials for full-time administration. Few prominent union leaders have sat in Labour cabinets; the most outstanding recent exceptions, Ernest Bevin and Frank Cousins, were recruited from outside Parlia-ment. When Mr Richard Crossman complained in 1957 that only four trade union MPs were fit for cabinet office he evoked much protest but no refutation.[27]

Since the 1920's the number of union-sponsored candidatures has fluctuated fairly narrowly between 120 and 140. Because most trade union candidatures are in safe seats, the proportion of sponsored MPs in the parliamentary party varies with the party's electoral fortunes.[28]

SPONSORED CANDIDATES {

DEFEATED

ELECTED

107

23

35
11

4

27

5

114

120

92

123

NON-SPONSORED CANDIDATES ELECTED

173

166

273

240

SPONSORED MP'S AS % OF TOTAL

40   76   30   36   34

FIGURE III. 2: Trade-union sponsorship of Labour Candidates

But although the number of union-sponsored Labour MPs is higher than ever before, the number of 'workers' (109) is considerably lower. The social revolution which the Parliamentary Labour Party has been undergoing has left its mark even on union nominations. Dr Jeremy Bray (Kingswood School, Cambridge and Harvard) is sponsored by the Transport and General Workers Union, Mr W. T. Rodgers (Quarry Bank School and Oxford) by the National Union of Municipal and General Workers, Mr Christopher Norwood (Whitgift School and Cambridge) by the Union of Shop, Distributive and Allied Workers.*

The narrow—and apparently narrowing—range from which parliamentary candidates, especially those in winnable seats, are chosen hardly entitles us to speak of a 'ruling class' in the accepted sense, or even of an oligarchy, if by oligarchy we mean a self-perpetuating clique. But it does point to the seemingly inevitable element of professionalism

*There is some precedent for these developments. Sidney Webb was sponsored by the Miners' Federation in 1922.

in modern representative politics, at all levels of activity from the cabinet to the ward committee. For the candidates themselves are chosen by selection committees which are unrepresentative in two important senses. In the first place, though the members of these committees owe their positions to supposedly democratic election by local party members, the actual management of the local party is in the vast majority of cases in the hands of a small band of devoted enthusiasts who constitute an oligarchy in the much stricter sense of the word.[29] Though nominally answerable to all local party members—often numbering many thousands—they are mostly able to act as if this were not so. Secondly, even if the rank-and-file members were disposed to exercise greater control they would still not comprise a cross-section of those who ultimately vote for the candidate. To a lesser extent than local party activists and to a much lesser extent than members of Parliament and, *a fortiori*, cabinet ministers, those who bother to enrol in a party at all are still an élite of sorts. Details studies in two widely separated boroughs bear this out overwhelmingly.

FIGURE III. 3: Supporters, Members and Officers of major Parties in Greenwich by social class (1950)

FIGURE III. 4: Supporters, Members and Officers of major Parties in Glossop (Derbyshire) by social class (1951-4)

The figures for both boroughs tell the same story. In all parties the higher the degree of political involvement, the greater the bias in favour of the higher social strata. The very poor are excluded from any activity except mere party membership. In the Labour Party the middle and lower middle classes gain at the expense of industrial workers; in the Conservative Party the business and professional classes gain even at the expense of white-collar workers.

Does it matter? The real importance of the selection process does not merely lie in the degree to which it limits the voter's choice. Selection amounts, in the vast majority of cases, to election. At least two-thirds of constituencies have been safe for one or other of the major parties since 1945. Seventy seats changed hands in 1964, fifty-three in 1966. Except in 1950 (when redistribution made direct comparison impossible) these have been the highest totals since the war.

CONSTITUENCY GOVERNMENT

In any election, therefore, about 90% of those elected to Parliament owe their good fortune not to the discrimination of the voters, but to the smoke-filled conclaves of between 50 and 200 largely self-appointed men and women. To this state of affairs there are two obvious objections. The first is one of principle—that here are people with too much power and too little responsibility. The second is pragmatic —that the type of person who makes these important decisions is not fit to make them.

'Constituency government [wrote Bagehot] is the precise opposite of parliamentary government. It is the government of immoderate persons far removed from the scene of action, instead of the government of moderate persons close to the scene of action.'[32]

Almost a century later Mr Nigel Nicolson, reflecting on his long drawn-out quarrel with the Bournemouth East constituency association, echoed that 'the party-battle, which is at least half a pretence in Parliament, has become a grim reality outside'.[33]

Those for whom party politics is the main hobby, perhaps even a passion, are surely more doctrinaire, more narrow-minded and more extremist than either casual party members or unattached voters. Their whole activity would make no sense if they lacked a conviction of the fundamental differences of principle which divide them from their opponents. This is certainly a widely held view, and the cartoonists' stereotypes of party activists are well known. Those who complain of excessive discipline in our political parties increasingly point to constituency militants rather than House of Commons whips as the villains. 'Loyalty' according to Mr Nicolson, 'is a word heard far less at Westminster than outside'.[34]

The main reason why oligarchical selection of candidates leads to less disastrous results than it might, is that this picture is largely false. True, MPs who deviate from the party line towards the centre tend to get a less friendly reception from their constituency organizations than those who deviate towards the extreme, but exceptions are numerous. At the time of Suez there were, among Conservative MPs, eight principal 'anti-Suez' rebels who abstained from a vote of confidence in the government on November 8, 1956, and eight principal 'pro-Suez' rebels who resigned the whip in May, 1957, when the government abandoned the British boycott of the canal. None of the 'pro-Suez' rebels suffered any inconvenience; of the 'anti-Suez' rebels three (Sir Robert Boothby, Sir Edward Boyle, Mr William Yates) escaped unscathed, but three others (Mr Nigel Nicolson, Sir Frank Medlicott and Col. Cyril Banks) were not re-adopted by their constituencies and, in addition, subjected to varying degrees of discourtesy.

The one 'pro-Suez' Labour rebel (Mr Stanley Evans) met such hostility from his local party that he also resigned his seat.[35]

Suez, it may be argued, is a special case which aroused exceptionally strong emotions, and Nigel Nicolson had compounded his difficulties with his local officials by having on an earlier occasion favoured the abolition of hanging. In contrast, of the twenty-seven 'Profumo' rebels who abstained from voting for the government on June 17, 1963, only one (Dr Donald Johnson) had serious difficulties with his constituency, although all but four of them had records of previous right-wing or centre deviations.[36] Before the 1966 election three 'liberal' Conservative MPs encountered difficulties with their associations, but overcame them. Mr Terence Higgins, Mr Richard Hornby and Mr Humphry Berkeley had all voted in favour of oil sanctions against Rhodesia and in favour of abolishing capital punishment. Mr Berkeley had also introduced a private member's bill to legalize adult homosexuality. These three were, however, a small proportion of Conservative 'liberals': a total of 31 Conservatives voted for oil sanctions, a total of 80 for Mr Silverman's 1965 bill on capital punishment, a total of 40 for a previous bill on homosexuality. On the other hand there was no local disapproval for any of the 55 'right wingers' who voted against oil sanctions in defiance of the party line, which was one of neutrality. In all, it is less comfortable to be a left-wing than a right-wing rebel in the Conservative Party, but even among left-wingers only a minority seem to suffer. It may be true that when Conservative candidates were deprived of their financial 'independence' in 1948 some power shifted from the MP to the caucus, but Professor McKenzie is unduly alarmist in concluding that while the leaders of the Conservative Party

'boast of the leniency and tolerance of their parliamentary discipline, they do not appear to have taken very active steps to warn their constituency zealots against exceeding their legitimate rôle in the political system.'[37]

The Labour Party presents a slightly different picture. Here the power of the whips is undoubtedly used more often, while the behaviour of constituency parties is less uniform. Constituency Labour Parties derive their reputation for left-wing extremism mainly from the success that 'Bevanites' have had in elections to the seven constituency seats on the National Executive Committee. It is also true that all the left-wing MPs who lost the whip in 1954 and 1961* continued to enjoy the confidence of their local parties. On the other hand two

*See above, p. 66.

of the four who were expelled in 1949 received no local support[38] and three prominent critics of nationalization, Sir Hartley Shawcross and Mr Richard Stokes in the 1950's, and Mr Desmond Donnelly more recently, experienced no difficulty. Only one MP was obliged to retire during the 1964 parliament—Mr William Warbey, a leading left-wing critic of the government's Viet-Nam policy. Most CLPs are subject to two conflicting pressures—on the one hand the desire to keep the Socialist faith pure, on the other loyalty to the movement and its leader. Mr Warbey's offence—and that of Conservative MPs who have made personal attacks on their leader—lies more in the act of disloyalty than in the ideological stance from which it is made.

If the majority of those local branches in both parties which deviate from the party line lean towards the extreme rather than the centre, most branches do not lean in any direction at all. Dr Richard Rose, who has studied the resolutions submitted to party conferences between 1955 and 1960, describes almost half the resolutions as 'non-partisan' (42% for Labour, 50% for Conservative). Half the Conservative associations submitted fewer than two resolutions in the five-year period; in both parties fewer than one quarter of the constituencies regularly press partisan views, fewer than one-fifth extreme partisan views.[39] The popular picture of militant constituency parties being consistently defeated by trade union block votes at Labour Party conferences is equally exaggerated. The only major issue since the war on which the party leadership has been saved by union votes was that of approving German re-armament in 1954.[40] In the crucial debates on unilateral disarmament at Scarborough and Blackpool in 1960–61 the leadership had the support of between 63 and 67% of CLPs.[41]

The reasons for this comparative lack of militancy are not mysterious. For many of those who join constituency parties loyalty to the national organization is the overriding emotion. Their general political outlook was probably formed by family background and social environment rather than conscious intellectual effort. The majority of them instinctively support the party's leaders, perhaps even with strongly-felt devotion. They accept the party's programme without always fully understanding it or even very detailed knowledge of it. The routine activities of local parties—fund-raising, garden fêtes, bingo, bazaars, outings—though ultimately devoted to political ends, are in themselves non-political. It is a mistake to think that even many 'activists' are primarily, let alone exclusively, obsessed by ideological controversy. They may be no more than conscientious citizens taking on a chore for which it is difficult to find volunteers.

If the pragmatic objection to constituency government is weak, there remains that based on principle: that in the great majority of constituencies the great majority of electors have no say in who is to become their representative. The remedy that is proposed is the 'primary', a mechanism evolved in the USA as a defence against boss-dominated 'machine politics'. On three occasions primaries have in fact taken place in Britain to settle disputes about Conservative candidatures, which in each case have confirmed the wishes of the association's executive committee.[42] One of these was in Bournemouth East and Christchurch, where the association's members voted by 3,762 to 3,671 not to re-adopt Nigel Nicolson, a decision which had previously been made by 298 votes to 92 at a meeting of the association and unanimously by the fifty-five member executive committee.[43] The discrepancy in these votes may seem to support the thesis that militants are more extreme than rank-and-file members;[44] whether it is valid to generalize from the unique circumstances of that episode is doubtful.

There is another difficulty. Even the large paid-up membership of the Bournemouth East Conservative Association was still a minority of the party's supporters,* let alone the whole electorate. In the United States a primary election can occasion a large turn-out; in one-party states (mainly the South), where the primary is effectively the election, turn-out is often higher than in the official election. This is possible because in order to participate an elector need only declare his allegiance when registering; he does not have to be a card-carrying member of a party. Some states, indeed, operate an 'open' primary, permitting any elector to vote in the primary of any one party. It is difficult to see British political parties extending this right to anyone other than full party members. The spread of the primary in the United States since the beginning of the century has undoubtedly reduced the power of some local and national oligarchs, though it has hardly transferred it 'from the politicians to the people'. It is difficult to dissent from H. J. Ford when he wrote, 'While bosses and machines may go, the boss and the machine are always with us'.[45] To which might be added that primaries, by doubling the number of campaigns, add to the cost of elections, to the advantage of the richer parties and the richer factions within them.

Candidate selection is the only segment of the British representational system in which constituency parties have played, and play, an active rôle. In all else, they are subordinate partners, though like many subordinates they can at times make their importance felt. In the planning of political campaigns and the determination of party policy the preponderant rôle goes to the national leaders.

*1959 figures: Electorate, 60,657; voters, 46,544; Conservative voters, 29,014; membership of association, 9,724; participants in primary, 7,433.

THE CONTINUITY OF ELECTIONS

The classical argument for the infrequency of elections is that it gives statesmen a respite from the importunities of the electorate; the five-year interval which has existed in Britain since the Parliament Act of 1911 is longer than in most parliamentary democracies. In quiet times the argument may have had some force. Parliamentary sessions were short, public interest in affairs of state limited and intermittent, the circulation of newspapers small, the outcome of elections, when they were contested, depended to a considerable extent on local conditions. This was true not merely until 1832, but largely until 1867. It was then that there began the permanent dialogue between electors and politicians. This was not merely because a mass electorate could only be reached by methods quite different from those of informal or aristocratic politics. The effect of the enfranchisement of the masses was the demand, however limited at first, for whole new areas of government activity. Once this was accepted by politicians, parliamentary sessions became longer, the subject-matter for discussion increased, mass-circulation newspapers, first published in the 1890's,* fed this interest, however crudely or inadequately. The political party became the two-way communication channel which it still is today: a means of justifying the actions of its leaders to the electors, and a means of discovering the wishes of the electors. There is, of course, nothing new in the actions of the government affecting the lives of the citizens. In previous centuries too, men have had to obey laws, pay taxes and fight wars. What is new is that those who govern are obliged to explain their actions (or inactivity) and to seek the citizen's approval.

The developments of the twentieth century have established the permanent dialogue even more firmly. On the one hand, the area of state activity has increased even further, thus strengthening the citizen's dependence on political events. On the other, the media of communication reach an even greater number of people. Almost everyone takes a newspaper, almost everyone has a radio or television set. Not everyone takes a deep interest in the political items; of those who do, by no means everyone acquires an accurate impression. That is beside the point. What matters is that almost every major event—the Budget, bank rate, the Trade Union Congress, a party conference, a summit trip—is accompanied by sensational publicity. Every weekend, outside the high summer, the politicians are out in force, making speeches. The long-term programme of almost every major govern-

*Evening News, 1894; Daily Mail, 1896; Daily Express, 1900; Daily Mirror, 1904.

ment department—housing, education, national insurance, regional development, not to mention a war,—affects most people continuously. It may be that only a minority would voluntarily turn their minds to political events, but the majority are seldom allowed to forget them. It is the sum total of these impressions and reactions which emerges as the voter's decision; it is the politicians' never-ceasing efforts to mould these reactions and impressions that constitute what Peel apprehensively foresaw as 'a perpetual vortex of agitation'.[46] Modern politics has been rightly described as a daily plebiscite.

The daily plebiscite becomes even more intense during the pre-election period. Before both the 1959 and 1964 elections poster and newspaper advertising began in earnest some eighteen months before polling day. The uncertainty concerning the date of the election added to the suspense in each case. After the 1964 election, which resulted in an overall Labour majority of four, it was obvious that another election was at most two years off, so that from the spring of 1963 to the spring of 1966 politics and government were dominated, not to say seriously interrupted, by electoral frenzy. In the eight years from 1958 to 1966, the atmosphere of at least four-and-a-half could be accurately described as pre-electoral. But whether the parliamentary majority is four or a hundred, it remains true that party leaders need to begin planning the next election as soon as polling day is over.

CAMPAIGN MANAGEMENT

The election campaign, as an enterprise co-ordinated by party headquarters, was slow to develop. The convention that campaigns are individual constituency events—on which the greater part of British electoral law is based to this day—survived to the beginning of the century. Sir Robert Peel's address to his constituents at Tamworth in 1834 is often referred to as the first party manifesto; it was certainly approved by the whole Cabinet and enunciated general principles of policy, but it did not formally commit any Conservative candidate at the subsequent election. Until 1867 at any rate, 'agitation' was the prerogative of extra-party associations, such as the Anti-Corn Law League. The first major statesman to stump the country was Gladstone in 1876-77 and again in 1879. But he was not at that time leader of the Liberal Party, and the major effort of his 1879 campaign was restricted to his own constituency of Midlothian. His innovation caused great distaste, Queen Victoria recoiling from the 'democratic rule of that half-mad fire-brand'.[47] It was imitated by his Radical rival, Joseph Chamberlain, but not by his Conservative contemporaries, Disraeli and Salisbury, or his Liberal successor, Rosebery. Attempts by the Radicals to impose a platform on the Liberal Party were only partly successful. The 'Newcastle Programme', drawn up by the National Liberal Federation in 1891, gained only qualified acceptance from Gladstone and the Federation never repeated even this limited success.

The Labour Party, founded in order to serve a particular purpose and based, in its earlier years, on collective leadership, had no difficulty in issuing official party manifestoes. Indeed, anything else would have been out of place. Its 1906 election address must therefore be regarded as the first of its kind in Britain. In the Conservative and Liberal parties, declarations by the leaders, though no longer directed only their own constituents, continued to function as manifestoes. As late as 1945 the Conservative election programme was entitled *Mr Churchill's Declaration of Policy to the Electors*.[48]

Conservativism in political practice, which is common to all the parties, meant that technical innovations in campaigning were few and slow in coming. Radio was first used in 1924 and became an accepted part of electioneering. In the marathon 1945 campaign each of the main parties had ten broadcasts and the Liberals four— a saturation of the ether not attempted since. Television was first used in 1951—on the initiative of the BBC, not of the parties[49]— when each party was allocated one programme. By 1959, when about 70% of the population owned sets, television had become the main medium of political communication, with the three parties giving five, five and two broadcasts respectvely. The party political programmes on Television had an average audience of 21%, while the sound broadcasts had one of only 3%. A total of 61% of the electorate— some twenty million people—claimed to have viewed at least one election programme.[50] 1959 was widely heralded as the 'TV election', though what this would imply was not clear. There was more apprehension than hope in this expectation: television offered more opportunity than any other medium for gimmickry, slickness and superficiality, and for gulling a clod-like electorate with cheap publicity tricks. These fears were not realized. Television, it turned out, had no more destroyed sane politics than it had destroyed the live theatre, professional football, the reading of novels or the art of conversation, the ruin of each of which had in turn been confidently prophesied. Indeed, the conclusion of the earliest researchers, in 1959, tended to discount the power of television to influence voting, and emphasized its educational qualities:

'There was a significant increase in political knowledge during the campaign . . . It seems . . . that the attempt to convey information does not meet with the same resistance as does the attempt to persuade,

F

but that material designed primarily to influence opinion may also increase knowledge ...

Political change was neither related to the degree of exposure nor to any particular programmes or argument put forward by the parties ...

The inter-election years become more important than the nineteen days of campaigning, however intensive, because the swing is almost entirely accounted for before the opening of the election campaign.'[51]

This assertion is misleading, however, because it refers only to the balance between the main contenders. Television can, during an election period, help minor parties which in normal times suffer from inadequate publicity. More intensive research in 1964 showed that the Liberals clearly profited in this way. Of those who switched their allegiance, more than half switched to the Liberal Party; more significantly, a pro-Liberal movement of opinion was highest amongst those who were not keenly interested in politics and who were therefore stimulated by the sudden rise in the propaganda and political news content of their normal viewing diet. Also, although the switches from one major party to another cancelled out, viewers were distinctly more aware of the themes the parties were emphasizing at the end of the campaign than at the beginning.[52] A similar development was noted in France during the presidential election of 1965, when M. Lecanuet, the last-minute Centre candidate, also profited from his television appearances.[53]

As a result of their 1959 experience, the broadcasting networks became more enterprising, and the parties less timorous, in their attitude to election reportage. In 1959 the only programmes not sponsored by the parties were Hustings (BBC) and Marathon (ITV). Programmes like Gallery, This Week and What the Papers Say were banished at a time when their relevance was greatest. In 1964 these programmes survived and Election Forum, in which the parties' leaders answered viewers' questions, proved more popular than any of the party broadcasts.[54] The networks are under an obligation to provide political balance, which the newspapers are manifestly not. But it is arguable that the parties still have too much power in deciding what constitutes balance, and one experienced observer remarked on the networks' 'jittery readiness to play unnecessarily safe'[55] even in 1966. The notion that the networks, unlike the press, exist to serve only the politicians' views of what should and should not be said may be dying, but we should also sympathize with the politician's fear that an election in which the studio producer had complete freedom might drown what the parties had to say.

If most of the technical improvements in television electioneering are due to the professional broadcasters, in other respects it is the parties who have been the innovators. Most leading politicians, having achieved their eminence by traditional methods, pride themselves on their instinctive ability to communicate, and their unique contact with the people's pulse. It was against these canons of intuitive campaigning that the Conservatives offended in 1957–59, by resorting for the first time to the professional public relations.[56] The firm of Colman, Prentis and Varley, which had briefly helped the party in 1949–51, was called in to plan an intensive newspaper and poster advertising campaign, in order to refurbish the party's public image after the Suez débacle and the economic deterioration. There followed a period of publicity unprecedented in both intensity and skill. The campaign stressed consumer prosperity, opportunity for all and Labour's negative and class-ridden approach. 'Life's better with the Conservatives. Don't let Labour ruin it', was one of the most effective slogans ever coined. But the power of professional persuaders to persuade should not be exaggerated. Most propaganda is successful only if it emphasizes what people are in any case willing to believe. If the evidence of prosperity had in 1959 been less patent, or the economy had suddenly taken a turn for the worse, the themes chosen by the Conservatives and their advisers would have back-fired badly. Experience in the 1964 campaign confirms this. In the first four months of that year the party spent nearly half a million pounds on projecting the personal image of Sir Alec Douglas-Home. During that period his NOP rating slumped from 58% to 48%.[57]

There were several reasons why the Conservatives were in a better position to pioneer this type of campaigning. In the first place it needs money. The Conservatives must have spent £468,000 in the 1958–59 pre-election period, compared with Labour's £103,000.[58] But Labour also had moral and aesthetic objections to commercializing politics at the expense of rational persuasion. Mr Crossman complained that the Prime Minister was being sold 'as though he were a detergent' and Mr Gaitskell thought 'the whole thing is somehow false'.[59] When a group of advertising men with Labour sympathies offered the party their services, they were rebuffed.[60]

Labour was, however, responsible for one major innovation in the 1959 campaign. Anxious to hit the headlines in what it judged to be a predominantly hostile press, it instituted a daily press conference. In the nature of things this advantage could last for only one election: by 1964 the Conservatives and Liberals had followed suit. It was the defeat in 1959, the fourth in succession and the worst, which revolutionized Labour's attitude to campaigning. It could no longer be claimed convincingly that Labour leaders instinctively knew what the majority of the public wanted. Clearly some of the issues raised by the party had failed to persuade: the manner in which they had been raised had failed to impress; worse still, some of the attitudes and priorities with which the party was associated, and which had once stood them in good stead, were no longer popular. Despite such objections as Mr Aneurin Bevan's that opinion polls 'took the poetry out of politics'[61] Labour was gradually converted to the need for market research techniques.

Accordingly between 1962 and 1964 Dr Mark Abrams of *Research Services* conducted a number of surveys in marginal constituencies to discover how voters viewed the rival parties, which issues they regarded as important, and how to identify what Dr Abrams called the 'target voters'. Professional journalists and advertising men also received a much warmer welcome than before 1959 and played a larger part in designing posters and devising such slogans as 'Let's GO with Labour' with the thumbs-up symbol. It is, of course, quite possible that Labour would have won the 1964 election even if its propaganda machine had been as amateurish as in the past. No-one can estimate the precise effect that Dr. Abrams' findings had on the course of the campaign, but one Labour official has remarked in retrospect. 'Those polls then were prodigiously influential though of course no-one will admit it now'.[62]

POLITICAL COMMUNICATION

Professionalism in political proganda has clearly come to stay. In this respect Britain has merely caught up with developments in the United States and a number of continental European states. It is a consequence of technical developments; it is also a consequence of the centralization of party organization and the 'nationalization' of political opinion—trends which highly-charged propaganda machines in turn further accelerate. But all political communication flows in two directions, even if it is easier for those in command of the machine to make their points than it is for ordinary voters or party members. Opinion polls, whether published or privately sponsored, can be a weapon in the hands of the ordinary citizen, by voicing grievances and establishing priorities which the party machine is either too sluggish or too out-of-touch to convey to headquarters. A specific example of this is the question of comprehensive schools. The Conservatives had originally planned to make opposition to comprehensives a major item in their 1966 campaign, until a survey revealed that their 'target voters' were in favour of them.[63]

The irruption of the persuasion industry into politics has given rise to a rather confused debate about the ethics of such methods. That political advertising, like all advertising, is open to abuse, is undeniable.

There *is* a danger that opinion could be manipulated, fears and phobias exploited and irrational sentiments generally excited by psychologically skilled 'salesmanship', though gifted demagogues in past generations have got by without the help of advertising agencies. There is, on the other hand, some hope that the possibilities of these techniques are limited. Smoothness, slickness and too-evident professionalism can evoke sales resistance. Sincerity and candour cannot be entirely simulated in a society which still respects these qualities. More than one heavily researched product has been a commercial flop; more than one professionally conducted campaign has resulted in defeat.

A second, and contradictory, objection is that politicians will become all too sensitive to the whims of public opinion. For ever scanning the poll charts, they will cease to act according to their principles and consciences and simply trim to whichever point of view is currently rating 51%. This particular objection merely re-states in a new form the central problem of democratic politics. Is the politician who consistently maintains his point of view steadfast and honest, or is he obstinate and arrogant? Is the assiduous reader of opinion polls a faithful servant of his constituents or an irresponsible weathercock? Was it magnanimous, or was it craven, of the Conservative Party to softpedal the comprehensive school issue even though they honestly believed selective education to be better? Was it conscientious, or merely incompetent, of Sir Alec Douglas-Home to emphasize the independent nuclear deterrent in 1964 when one survey after another showed that defence policy came at the bottom of most voters' order of importance?

Professional electioneering is necessarily expensive electioneering. Characteristically, British election law is still based on the same assumptions as the Corrupt and Illegal Practices Act of 1883 which first seriously limited election expenses—namely, that it is the campaign in the constituencies, and the risk of bribery by individual candidates, which are decisive. The legal limits at present imposed on candidates have remained unchanged since 1950,* despite steeply rising printing costs. Most candidates spend suspiciously near the permitted maximum, which is a tribute more to their agents' accounting skill than to their honesty. A few candidates, if they are fighting safe seats or are confident of their personal popularity, are much more frugal. Mr Albert Evans retained South-West Islington for Labour for less than £300 in both 1964 and 1966;[64] Mr James Maxton (ILP) held Glasgow, Bridgeton for £165 in 1945, no doubt a record in modern times.[65]

*In borough constituencies, £450 plus 1½d per elector. In county constituencies, £450 plus 2d per elector. (Great Britain only; N. Ireland has a lower scale).

Constituency expenditure, 1966[66]

	Total	Per candidate	% of maximum
	£	£	£
Conservative	480,000	766	89
Labour	450,000	726	90
Liberal	150,000	501	56
Others	50,000	338	41

The danger in the 1960's, however, is not that the electors will be drowned in 'a torrent of gin and beer' (to which Gladstone attributed the Liberal defeat of 1874),[67] but that they will be suffocated by a surfeit of posters and newsprint. Labour Party expenditure on nation-wide pre-election publicity trebled between 1959 and 1964, that of Conservative Party more than doubled.

Pre-election publicity expenditure, 1959–64[68]

	1959	1964
	£	£
Labour	103,000	314,000
Conservative	468,000	992,000

Even more significant were the sums spent by such bodies as the Iron and Steel Federation, Aims of Industry and the Economic League in order to influence the electorate. These organizations claim to be non-partisan and their propaganda tends to be restricted to a single issue (nationalization) rather than the whole range of policy. But it is evident that such publicity favours the Conservatives at the expenses of Labour. In 1959 it cost an estimated £1,435,000, in 1964 an estimated £1,896,000, one-and-a-half times the total spent in all constituency campaigns. Neither these sums nor the costs of party advertising count as 'election expenses', though if money brings any political returns at all, it is this, and not the local candidate's photograph, that matters. Nor are there any proposals to limit spending by the parties nationally or by outside bodies. Changes to the Companies Act, proposed by the Labour Government, would compel companies to reveal political contributions; this, if enacted, could reduce the Conservative Party's income. What proportion of Conservative funds emanate from industrial sources is not known: the party does not publish its accounts. The Labour Party has since the war derived about two-thirds of its central income and one-third of constituency income from affiliation fees by trade unions.[69] In addition, most unions make *ad hoc* grants to the general election fund, for which the party is almost entirely dependent on union generosity.[70] Recently, however, the Labour Party has been making greater efforts to 'live of its own', by organizing competitions and lotteries and soliciting its better-off supporters.

ARE CAMPAIGNS EFFECTIVE?

The growing centralization of campaigning means that it is the national, not the local propaganda which matters. Radio and television, advertising and newspaper reports have largely displaced the more traditional forms of electioneering. It is the slogans, quips and fauxpas of the party leaders, not of the individual candidate, that set the tone of debate. The local meeting is not dead, but it increasingly takes place at a factory gate or a shopping arcade rather than in an infant school or a dingy hall. The candidate can no longer summon his audience, he has to seek it out. An itinerant party leader can still, of course, draw a huge audience, but to the local standard-bearer a star speaker is a mixed blessing who may merely emphasize the anticlimax of his own effort. Increasingly the local candidate is merely the mouthpiece for the party's policy, not the advocate of his own personality.

The golden age of the pamphlet and the fly-sheet is over. In 1895 the Liberal Party distributed 23 million leaflets, four per elector.[71] The Labour Party's *Signposts for the Sixties*, an exceptionally well produced document published in 1961, did well to sell a million copies.[72] Their impact is hard to measure;* it is probably greater inside the party, where they can educate about new policies and provide speakers with material, than outside. Meetings, other than those with star billings, probably serve the same purpose. They raise morale and they given an impression of activity. Because they are mainly attended by the faithful they do not persuade. But the faithful are often 'opinion leaders' in their community, and the meeting equips them to pass on arguments and impressions to colleagues and neighbours.

As in quieter times the activities of the local party machine are largely administrative: their purpose is political, but their content is not. Canvassing, the hiring of halls, the addressing of envelopes and the manning of committee rooms require no ideological sophistication. They do require efficiency. The purpose of canvassing is not primarily to convert. It is partly a courtesy: if one wants a person's vote, one might at least call on him. But its main purpose is to locate supporters, especially those who might need transport on polling day or who have moved since the register was drawn up. Whether efficient organization can win elections is disputed. For the past four elections

*'Who reads the leaflets, apart from the Oxford dons who write book elections, is not known'. (Jennings, *Party Politics*, Vol. I, p. 226.)

the authors of the Nuffield studies have asked the parties to name in advance those constituencies where organization had most improved. The results in these constituencies deviated only negligibly from the rest.[73] This is not in itself conclusive. The sample is small and parties presumably concentrate their improvements in marginal seats, so that some of the improvements might cancel out. There are two other indices which suggest that organization can make a difference. They are the size of the turn-out and the size of the postal vote.

Since 1959 at any rate there has been a marked difference in turn-out in safe and marginal seats. In the country as a whole turn-out dropped by 3% from 78.8% to 75.8%. Between 1964 and 1966 it dropped by 1.2% But in marginal seats (i.e. those where the Conservatives had got between 47½ and 55% of the major-party vote) it *rose* by 1.4%;* in seats which Conservatives had held by less than 1% it rose by 2.3%.[74] It may be that electors in these constituencies were so conscious of their crucial rôle that they needed no further prodding to go out and vote. But this is not very plausible. Those who hover between voting and abstaining are more apathetic and less well-informed than habitual voters;** it is much more likely that some at least of the extra turn-out (which in a few cases bordered on the spectacular***) was due to efficient dragooning. The fact that the *swing* in such constituencies did not differ markedly from the rest of the country is no disproof. If Daz and Omo both step up their advertising equally, their shares of the market will not change much. But Daz dare not let up, lest Omo then gain an advantage.

The postal vote provides a much more clear-cut opportunity for organizational superiority. The 1948 Act permitted the chronically-sick, those who had moved and those absent on business to vote by post. In the 1964 election the average postal vote in Conservative-won seats was 1,601, in Labour-won seats 1,003. That in itself does not prove that the Conservative party is more efficient at organizing those entitled to a postal vote: evidence from other countries suggests that this facility favours more middle-class than working-class electors and

*To some extent this rise in turn-out is 'technical': the 1966 register was more up-to-date than that of 1964. But this is not important. What matters is the *difference* in behaviour between safe and marginal seats.

**See below, pp. 117.

*** Constituency	1964 majority	1964–66 increase in turn-out
Brighton, Kemptown	Lab. 7	7·9%
Leyton	Con. 205 (by-election)	5·9%
Eton & Slough	Con. 11	5·3%
Hampstead	Con. 1,835	4·8%
Reading	Con. 10	4·2%

is therefore a bonus to right-wing parties.[75] What is significant is that in the nine most marginally won Conservative seats in 1964 the average postal vote was 1,772.[76] Postal ballots are not counted separately, but the overwhelming impression of party agents is that in marginal seats they help the Conservatives. On the assumption that they split 2:1 in favour of the Conservatives, they would have been decisive in twelve constituencies; at any other election since 1950 they would have been decisive in at least six constituencies.

It is one thing to dragoon, another to persuade. Canvassers and knockers-up have to go on the assumption that most people's minds are made up: an election campaign makes sense only on the assumption that some are not. It is frequently claimed that the campaign itself influences nobody: opinions are changed, if at all, in the course of a government's lifetime, not in the final hectic three weeks. As we have seen, under modern political conditions electioneering never stops. The dissolution of Parliament does not mark a beginning in the onslaught on the voters' favours, merely a change in its intensity. To that extent the voter's decision is the outcome of a host of impressions accumulated over a number of years. On the other hand opinion polls have shown some movement of opinion during all of the post-war election campaigns; except in 1955 and 1964* the trend was for the gap between the main parties to narrow. Old loyalties were being re-asserted. Whether it was the campaign oratory or the mere proximity of polling day which had this effect cannot be proved. But if the speeches, posters and canvassers have no other effect, they at least remind people that there is an election on.

In the last resort that is the only claim that can be made on behalf of election campaigns and indeed party activity generally. They can mobilize and they can inform. They can stimulate into temporary activity those men and women for whom public affairs are not a primary and overriding concern. There is a small minority who become permanently involved in politics for a variety of personal reasons[77] and for whom political activity can become an end in itself, perhaps even an obsession. But even that larger minority who are prepared to belong to parties and lend a hand at election times have to be kept together, and sometimes even recruited, by the prospect of social or cultural activities which have little to do with the aims of the parties.† An

---

*In 1955 the Conservative lead increased slightly. In 1964 the various polls showed contradictory trends, roughly cancelling each other out.

†Cf. the claim, 'In the Young Conservatives it is not all Politics; far from it . . . ', quoted by Milne & Mackenzie, *Marginal Seat*, p. 14. Twelve years later the prose style has changed, but not the message: 'A cool approach to hot ideas makes for a big, big leisure scene. Make the pace, set the style as a Young Conservative'. (1966 leaflet).

election, and an election campaign, bring citizens into contact with the machinery of the government and with individual politicians in a way for which there are otherwise few opportunities. This participation is of great psychological importance to the citizen. It gives him a stake in his system of government, offers him a chance to affirm his loyalties, and symbolizes his constitutional rights. The best testimony to this comes from totalitarian states with one-party systems. Their 'elections' in which 99.9% of the electorate vote for the government list are regarded as a joke in western countries. Yet régimes would hardly bother with them if the ritual of elections served no other purpose than the expression of policy choices.

REFERENCES

CHAPTER III

1. Gash, N. *Politics in the Age of Peel. A Study in the Technique of Parliamentary Representation, 1830-50* (London, 1953), pp. 393-409.
2. *Ibid.*, p. 441.
3. Hanham, H. J. *Elections and Party Management, Politics in the Time of Disraeli and Gladstone* (London, 1959), p. 197.
4. Beer, *Modern British Politics*, p. 263.
5. *Ibid.*, pp. 257, 262.
6. McKenzie, R. T. *British Political Parties. The Distribution of Power within the Conservative and Labour Parties* (2nd edn., London, 1963), p. 146.
7. Beer, *op. cit.*, p. 52.
8. McKenzie, *op. cit.*, p. 468.
9. Critchley, J. 'Government by Greengrocer' ('Candidates: How They Pick Them') *New Statesman*, February 5, 1965.
10. Beer, *op. cit.*, p. 258.
11. Ranney, A. *Pathways to Parliament. Candidate Selection in Britain* (London, 1965), pp. 21-4, 26-7.
12. *Ibid.*, p. 53.
13. McKenzie, *op. cit.*, p. 474 n.
14. Harrison, M. *Trade Unions and the Labour Party Since 1945* (London, 1960), pp. 80-88.
15. *Ibid.*, p. 81.
16. Ranney, *op. cit.*, pp. 74, 181.
17. Schattschneider, E. E. *Party Government*, p. 64.
18. Butler, D. E. *The British General Election of 1951* (London, 1952), p. 41; Butler & King, *The British General Election of 1966*, pp. 208, 210.

19, 20. Ross J. F. S. *Elections and Electors. Studies in Democratic Representation* (London, 1955), pp. 415-7; Nicholas, H. G. *The British General Election of 1950* (London, 1951), pp. 46-7; Butler, D. E., *op. cit.*, p. 39; Butler, D. E. *The British General Election of 1955* (London, 1955), p. 42; Butler, D. E. & Rose, R. *The British General Election of 1959* (London, 1960), p. 128; Butler, D. E. & King, A. S. *The British General Election of 1964* (London, 1965), p. 237; Butler & King, *The British General Election of 1966*, p. 208.

21. Butler & King, *The British General Election of 1966*, p. 210; Guttsman, W. L. *The British Political Elite* (London, 1963), pp. 104-5.

22. Ranney, *op. cit.*, p. 112.

23. Critchley, *loc. cit.*

24. Butler, *General Election of 1951*, pp. 38, 41; Butler & Rose, *General Election of 1959*, pp. 126, 127; Butler & King, *General Election of 1966*, pp. 207, 209.

25. Butler, *General Election of 1951*, p. 38; Butler, *General Election of 1955*, p. 41; Butler & Rose, *op. cit.*, p. 129; Butler & King, *General Election of 1964*, p. 238; Butler & King, *General Election of 1966*, p. 209.

26. Halévy, E. *History of the English People in the Nineteenth Century*, Vol. VI (2nd edn., London, 1952), p. 65.

27. Harrison, *op. cit.*, p. 269.

28. *Ibid.*, pp. 265-7.

29. Cf. Casinelli, C. W. 'The Law of Oligarchy', *American Political Science Review* XLVII (September, 1953).

30. Benney, M., Gray, A. P. & Pear, R. E. *How People Vote* (London, 1956), pp. 47, 51, 102-3.

31. Birch, A. H. *Small-Town Politics* (Oxford. 1959), p. 81.

32. Bagehot, *The English Constitution*, p. 161.

33. Nicolson, N. *People and Parliament* (London, 1958), p. 169.

34. *Ibid.*, p. 75.

35. Epstein, L. D. *British Politics in the Suez Crisis* (London, 1964), pp. 98-119.

36. Rasmussen, J. S. *The Relations of the Profumo Rebels with their Local Parties* (Tuscon, Arizona, 1966), pp. 30-40, 42, 53.

37. McKenzie, *op. cit.*, p. 634.

38. Ranney, *op. cit.*, pp. 158-9, 182-3.

39. Rose, R. 'The Policy Ideas of English Party Activists', *American Political Science Review* LVI (June, 1962), pp. 365-6; reprinted in Rose, *Studies in British Politics. A Reader in Political Sociology* (London, 1966), pp. 293-7.

40. Harrison, *op. cit.*, p. 229; McKenzie, *op. cit.*, p. 502.

41. Hindell, K. & Williams, P. M. 'Scarborough and Blackpool: An Analysis of Some Votes at the Labour Party Conferences of 1960 and 1961', *Political Quarterly* XXXIII (July, 1962), p. 331.

42. Ranney, *op. cit.*, pp. 62-5.

43. Martin, L. W. 'The Bournemouth Affair: Britain's First Primary Election', *Journal of Politics* XXII (November, 1960), pp. 661, 679.

44. This is argued by McKenzie, *op. cit.*, p. 632.
45. Quoted by Key, *Politics, Parties and Pressure Groups*, p. 395.
46. Quoted by White, R. J. *The Conservative Tradition* (London, 1950), p. 157.
47. Magnus, Sir P. *Gladstone. A Biography* (London, 1954), p. 270.
48. McCallum, R. B. & Readman, A. *The British General Election of 1945* (Oxford, 1947), p. 47.
49. Butler, *General Election of 1951*, p. 75.
50. Butler & Rose, *op. cit.*, pp. 92-3.
51. Trenaman, J. & McQuail, D. *Television and the Political Image* (London, 1961), pp. 232, 128.
52. Blumler J. G. & McQuail, D. *Election Television in the 1960s* (London, 1967), Chapter VIII. Dr Blumler has kindly lent me the manuscript of this book.
53. *Revue Française de Science Politique* XVI (February, 1966), p. 188.
54. Butler & King, *General Election of 1964*, p. 162.
55. Butler & King, *General Election of 1966*, p. 128.
56. For a detailed account of this campaign, see Lord Windlesham, *Communication and Political Power* (London, 1966), Chapter 3.
57. Rose, R. *Influencing Voters. A Study of Campaign Rationality* (London, 1967), pp. 58, 181.
58. Butler & Rose, *op. cit.*, pp. 21, 28.
59. *Ibid.*, pp. 20, 27 n.
60. *Ibid.*, p. 25.
61. Butler and King, *General Election of 1964*, pp. 50-1.
62. Butler & King, *General Election of 1966*, p. 33.
63. *Ibid.*, p. 93.
64. Butler & King, *General Election of 1964*, p. 228; *General Election of 1966*, p. 203.
65. McCallum & Readman, *op. cit.*, p. 297.
66. Butler & King, *General Election of 1966*, p. 203.
67. Morley, J. *Life of Gladstone* (London, 1903), Vol. II, p. 475.
68. Butler & Rose, *op. cit.*, pp. 21, 28; Butler & King, *General Election of 1964*, pp, 372, 374.
69. Harrison, *op. cit.*, pp. 72, 99.
70. *Ibid.*, pp. 66-7.
71. Ostrogorski, M. *Democracy and the Organisation of Political Parties* (London, 1902), Vol. I. p. 408, n. 1.
72. Butler & King, *General Election of 1964*, p. 64.
73. *Ibid.*, p. 295; *General Election of 1966*, p. 263.
74. Butler & King, *General Election of 1966*, p. 285.
75. Cf. Germany: *Wirtschaft und Statistik*, January, 1962, p. 25, January, 1966, p. 40.
76. Butler & King, *General Election of 1964*, p. 226.
77. Cf. Lane, R. E. *Political Life. Why and How People Get Involved in Politics* (2nd edn., New York, 1964); Milbrath L. W. *Political Participation*, (Chicago, 1965).

Voting Behaviour

ALTHOUGH an election is a ritual which involves much beside the making of choices, it is also a choice; indeed, some languages have only one word for the two processes. What we think about the merits of making political choices by means of elections depends on what we think of our fellow-citizens' capacity for making choices.

Most nineteenth-century advocacy of an extended franchise rested on the asumption that voters are capable of choosing rationally, though even the most advanced liberal theorists, like James and John Stuart Mill, admitted that the least educated were least equipped to do so. At the beginning of this century Lord Bryce stipulated a more modest requirement, the 'average man',

'The man of broad common sense, mixing on equal terms with his neighbours, forming a fair unprejudiced judgment on every question, not viewy or pedantic like the man of learning, nor arrogant like the man of wealth, but seeing things in a practical, businesslike, and withal kindly spirit, pursuing happiness in his own way, and willing that everyone else should do so. Such average men make the bulk of the people, and are pretty sure to go right, because the publicity secured to the expression of opinion by speech and in print will supply them with ample materials for judging what is best for all . . .

He may have limited knowledge and no initiative, yet he may be able to form . . . a shrewd judgment of men . . . What he lacks in knowledge he often makes up for by a sympathetic comprehension of the attitude of his fellow-men.'[1]

The foundations of such assumptions have been pretty thoroughly undermined by the progress of two modern disciplines, psychology and sociology. As a result we know much more about why people hold the political views that they do, though the implications for representational theory are by no means clear-cut.

Before we ask *why*, it is best to ask *how*. The raw material of voting behaviour is in the voting figures (See Table on page 96). At the parliamentary level, these shifts in voting have led to great variations in representation. But then, the British electoral system is notorious for exaggerating the effects of such shifts. The chief impression which the voting figures convey is one of stability, not volatility. Figure IV.1 shows that since the war neither of the major parties has gained less than 39.7% of the total vote or more than 49.3%. (For the sake of simplicity Northern Ireland and the university constituencies are excluded throughout this chapter). The contrast with the United States is striking (Figures IV.1, IV.2). Only once, in 1945, has the gap between the two main parties in Britain exceeded 7%. The movement from election to election has also been small. This movement is normally measured in terms of 'net swing', which can be calculated in a variety of ways.[2] The most widely used* and most easily

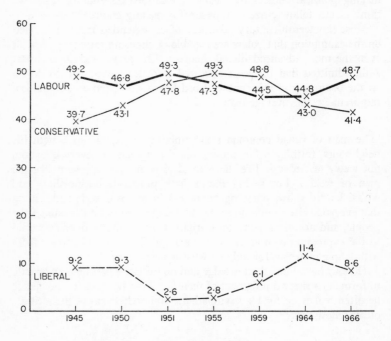

FIGURE IV. 1: Percentage of total vote by Party, 1945–66 (Great Britain only)

*e.g. in the Nuffield College election studies, *The Times Guide to the House of Commons, The Economist* and by both broadcasting networks.

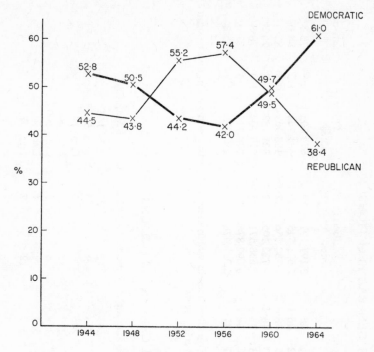

TABLE IV. 2: Percentage of total vote by Presidential candidates in USA,
1944–64

comprehensible, although also the crudest, is to average the percentage
gain by one major party and percentage loss by the other, e.g.

$$\text{Example 1} \begin{cases} \text{Party A:} & + 5\% \text{ of all votes cast} \\ \text{Party B:} & - 5\% \text{ of all votes cast} \\ \text{Party Z:} & \pm 0\% \text{ of all votes cast} \end{cases}$$

$$\text{Swing} = 5\%$$

$$\text{Example 2} \begin{cases} \text{Party A:} & + 2\% \text{ of all votes cast} \\ \text{Party B:} & - 7\% \text{ of all votes cast} \\ \text{Party Z:} & + 5\% \text{ of all votes cast} \end{cases}$$

$$\text{Swing} = \frac{2 + 7}{2} = 4\tfrac{1}{2}\%$$

VOTES CAST IN BRITISH GENERAL ELECTIONS, 1945–66

	Electorate	Conservative votes	%	Labour votes	%	Liberal votes	%	Other votes	%	Turn-out %
1945*	32,836,419	9,577,667	39·8	11,632,891	48·3	2,197,101	9·1	674,703	2·8	73·3
1950	34,269,770	12,502,567	43·5	13,266,592	46·1	2,621,548	9·1	381,964	1·3	84·0
1951	34,645,573	13,717,538	48·0	13,948,605	48·8	730,556	2·5	198,969	0·7	82·5
1955	34,858,263	13,311,936	49·7	12,404,970	46·4	722,405	2·7	321,182	0·2	76·8
1959	35,397,080	13,749,830	49·4	12,215,538	43·8	1,638,571	5·9	275,304	1·0	78·8
1964	35,892,572	12,001,396	43·4	12,205,814	44·1	3,092,878	11·2	348,914	1·3	77·0
1966	35,966,975	11,418,413	41·9	13,056,951	47·9	2,327,470	8·5	456,909	1·7	75·8

*Voting figures adjusted to allow for double-member constituencies in which electors had two votes each, and to omit university seats.

SEATS WON IN BRITISH GENERAL ELECTIONS, 1945–66

	Total	Conservative	Labour	Liberal	Others	Overall Majority
1945	640	213	393	12	22	Lab. 146
1950	625	298	315	9	3	Lab. 5
1951	625	321	295	6	3	Con. 17
1955	630	345	277	6	2	Con. 60
1959	630	365	258	6	1	Con. 100
1964	630	303	317	9	1	Lab. 4
1966	630	253	363	12	2	Lab. 97

On this calculation, the purpose of which is to isolate that section of the electorate which seems to have changed its mind, the swing at post-war elections has been

1950 2·9% to Con.
1951 1·1% to Con.
1955 1·8% to Con.
1959 1·1% to Con.
1964 3·1% to Lab.
1966 2·7% to Lab.

In 1951, 1955, 1966 over half the constituencies had a swing which was within 1% of the national average, though in 1959 and 1964 the divergence was rather greater. This consistency is in keeping with the social and ideological homogeneity which have already been noted. Its development has accompanied—both as cause and as consequence —the rise of the modern disciplined political party, but it has become overwhelmingly true of British politics only since the establishment of the Labour-Tory duel. Up to the First World War changes determined by local conditions and going against the tide were common. In January, 1910, when the Conservatives gained 128 seats, Liberals and their Labour allies were still able to gain thirteen seats that they had failed to capture in the landslide of 1906. The second election of that year, in December, led to virtually the same overall result*, but fifty-six seats changed hands.[3] Since the war the greatest number of seats to change hands against the tide was six (in 1959); in 1950, 1951 and 1966 there were none at all. 1959 was also the only post-war election in which more than one-sixth of the seats showed swings in the opposite direction from the general trend. Only since the war have both major parties attempted to cover the entire country. 1950 was the first election in which all constituencies outside Northern Ireland were contested, with Labour candidates in every seat (except the Speaker's) in England, Scotland and Wales. It was not until 1964 that the Conservatives followed suit. The elimination of the Independent MP is also a post-war phenomenon. As late as 1945 territorial constituencies returned two Communists, one ILP and seven Independents against the opposition of the major parties. Of the Independents, four were party rebels, the other three 'genuine' non-party men. Except for the ILP members who had joined the Labour Party they were all defeated in 1950. Since then no Independent or minor party candidate has been elected, or come anywhere near it, at a general election, but one Welsh Nationalist has been successful at a by-election.

*	Conservative	Liberal	Labour	Irish
January, 1910	273	275	40	82
December, 1910	272	272	42	84

G

It is, no doubt, possible to exaggerate the firmness of British party loyalties. Not only opinion polls but by-elections and municipal elections show that the limits within which opinion can move are quite wide. Between 1959 and 1964 Gallup recorded a maximum Conservative lead of 13% in October, 1960, just after the Scarborough conference, and a maximum Labour lead of 20% in June, 1963, just after Mr Profumo's resignation.[4] National Opinion Poll, the other main polling organization, showed the following maximum fluctuations:[5]

	Conservative	Labour	Liberal
	%	%	%
August, 1960	50	39	11
March, 1962	29	33	38
June, 1963	33	52	15

Opinion polls, though accurate enough as guides to the direction in which opinion is moving, are not so accurate that any one sample can be taken literally. The extreme points in the parties' popularity came immediately after spectacular events—Labour's defence split, the Orpington by-election, the Profumo affair—and receded fairly quickly. At the same time, it is evident that the number of *potentially* volatile voters is much greater than those who appear to have actually changed their minds at an election.

If party loyalty is as strong as the election figures suggest, then it is clear that most electors are not, as rationalist utopians once thought, in a state of perpetual choice. On the contrary, most political allegiance seems to be a matter of habit, and it is here that the psychologists' and sociologists' explanations become relevant. What determines these habits of allegiance? Family influence, class, region, religion, sex and age all play their party, though these categories do not fall into watertight compartments. Easily the most important of all is class. Class is the basis of British party politics; all else is embellishment and detail.

CLASS AND PARTY

Until the middle of the nineteenth century 'connection' and local influence were as powerful as any other factors in determining party loyalty, the more so as the parties themselves had neither easily recognizable policies nor coherent internal organization. Over the last hundred years, however, class and party have increasingly coincided. Especially since the Second Reform Act 1867, the further one went down the social scale, the more likely one was to find support for the party of the left (Liberal until 1914, Labour thereafter). This is more easily established for the years before the ballot than after. An examination of the poll books, in which every voter's preference was recorded, shows the following results for two typical constituencies.

Rochdale, 1857[6]

	Liberal	Conservative
Drink interest	28	118
Capitalists	34	54
Craftsmen	133	95
Retailers	167	102
Professional & dependants	88	106
Others	36	54
	480	527

Cambridge, 1868[7]

	Liberal	Conservative
Craftsmen	809	393
Labourers	289	123
Servants	90	235

How is class measured? Occupation and income are the most obvious criteria and to a large extent they overlap, but occupation is the more reliable of the two. The simplest course is to divide society into 'middle' and 'working' class (or manual and non-manual). The great majority of people, when asked to place themselves socially, use one of these two categories (or some fairly obvious equivalent, such as 'professional' or 'labouring') rather than any of the more refined sub-divisions that a social scientist would prefer. But simplicity is sometimes achieved at the expense of over-simplification: a division of society into two is not as easy as Marx and Engels once imagined it to be.* To use only two classes involves arbitrary decisions about the dividing line. This may not matter much if one simply wants to demonstrate that in general party goes with class, or to plot long-term developments in the relationship. But it becomes a serious obstacle if one wants to identify sub-groups, such as working-class Conservatives and middle-class Socialists. For this reason social investigators tend to use more elaborate scales. The first of these is an adaptation of the one used by the Registrar-General since 1911,[8] with a sub-division in the largest and most heterogeneous of the five clases, C (Routine white-collar and

*'Our epoch, the epoch of the bourgeoisie, possesses . . . this distinctive feature: it has simplified the class antagonisms. Society is more and more splitting up into two great hostile camps, into two great classes directly facing each other—bourgeoisie and proletariat.' (*Communist Manifesto*, 1848).

skilled manual). This scale is used by the Institute of Practitioners in Advertising and most market research organizations, and by NOP (National Opinion Polls).

The Gallup Poll uses a slightly different scale:

NOP	IPA		GALLUP	
12% AB	A Higher managerial, administrative or professional		Average + / well-to-do	6%
	B Intermediate managerial, administrative or professional		Average/upper middle and middle class	22%
22% C1	C1 Supervisory, clerical; junior managerial, administrative or professional			
37% C2	C2 Skilled manual workers		Average-/lower middle and working class	61%
29% DE	D Semi-skilled and unskilled manual workers			
	E State pensioners, casual workers		Very poor	11%

The third is the Hall-Jones scale which uses seven categories:[10]

1. Professional and high administrative, e.g. surgeon, chartered accountant;
2. Managerial and executive, e.g. personnel manager, primary school headmaster;
3. Higher-grade inspectional, supervisory and other non-manual, e.g. police inspector, farm bailiff;
4. Lower-grade inspectional, supervisory and other non-manual, e.g. insurance agent, costing clerk, tobacconist;
5. Skilled manual and routine non-manual, e.g. compositor, drapery shop assistant;
6. Semi-skilled manual, e.g. assembly worker, butcher's shop assistant;
7. Unskilled manual.

This has the advantage of combining 'objective' with 'subjective' assessment, since Hall and Caradog-Jones conducted a survey to discover the status which various occupations enjoy.*

*The reliability of this scale has been disputed. See D. V. Glass (ed.) *Social Mobility in Britain*, ch. 2, and M. Young & P. Willmott, 'Social Grading by Manual Workers,' *British Journal of Sociology*, VII (December, 1956).

The most recent attempt to locate as exactly as possible the elusive dividing line between 'middle' and 'working' class has been made by Butler and Stokes who, using the market-research/registrar-general classification, found that class CI (lower non-manual) straddled this line, both in the self-assessment of those who belonged to it and in objectively observable habits. At the top this class (telegraph operators, qualified local authority officers, secretaries and typists with subordinates, draughtsmen) 60% classed themselves as 'middle'; as many as 20% took a quality newspaper (*The Times, Guardian* or *Daily Telegraph*). At the bottom of the class (shop assistants, policemen, transport inspectors, lodging housekeepers) only 32% classed themselves as 'middle' and only 5% read a quality newspaper.[11] As Figure IV.3 shows, the drop in self-assessed status between C1a and C1b is greater than that between any other two classes, though the sharpest break in political support occurs between C1b and C2. Whether this marginal category is attributed to the broader 'middle' or 'working' classes makes a great difference to the correlation between social status and party affiliation. If it counts as middle (as is usually done, since its members are non-manual) then the two parties show degrees of class support which are almost mirror-images.

FIGURE IV. 3: Self-attributed middle-class status and Party preference by classes (Summer, 1963)

Party support by class, counting C1b as 'middle' (Summer 1963)

	Middle	Working
Conservative	77%	27%
Labour	23%	73%

If, on the other hand, it is consigned to the working class, as most of its members seem to think it should be, the imbalance in class support becomes considerable: [12]

Party support by class, counting C1b as 'working' (Summer 1963)

	Middle	Working
Conservative	80%	32%
Labour	20%	68%

These details apart, the general picture, reinforced by the opinion poll data in Figures IV.4 and IV.5, is a familiar one. People in manual occupations—however defined—are, in the majority, Labour; those who are not are, in the majority, Conservative. This 'obvious' observation requires two qualifications. Class is by no means the only plausible criterion for party cleavage in a modern state; it is true, however, that British party politics are more highly class-bound than those in most other countries. A recent comparison between four Anglo-Saxon democracies (Britain, USA, Canada, Australia) showed that of the four Britain had the highest* index of class voting.[13] This index is constructed by subtracting the percentage of non-manual workers voting for the party of the Left from the percentage of manual workers who do so, thus revealing the gap between the classes, e.g.

% voting for Left party

Manual:	75
Non-manual:	25
Index of class voting:	+50

A high index may therefore be achieved when most manual workers vote Left and most non-manual workers do not. A lower index may result *either* from many manual workers voting Right (e.g. Western Germany),[14] *or* from many non-manual workers voting Left (e.g. Norway);[15] an even lower or negative index when both happen (e.g. Canada).[16]

This makes the second qualification important. Class voting in Britain may be high, but it is by no means as high as it might be. Most

*But there is some evidence that it is as high in New Zealand as in Britain. (Chapman, Jackson & Mitchell, *New Zealand Politics in Action*, pp. 175-6.)

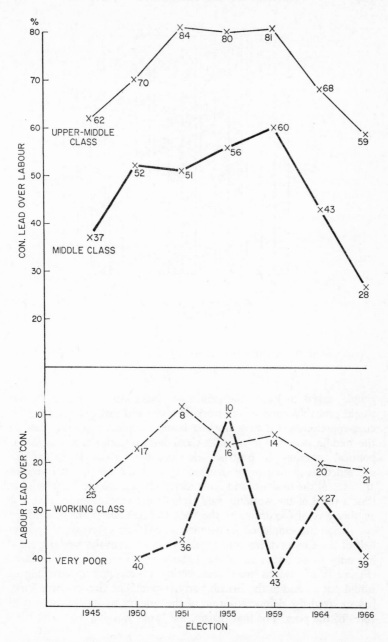

FIGURE IV. 4: Party preference by class, 1945–66 (Gallup poll)

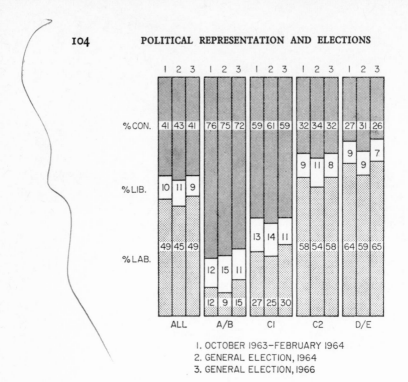

I. OCTOBER 1963–FEBRUARY 1964
2. GENERAL ELECTION, 1964
3. GENERAL ELECTION, 1966

FIGURE IV. 5: Party preference by class, 1963–66 (N.O.P.)

people, asked to locate the centre of class-consciousness in Britain would probably point to the working class; and this is correct in that class-consciousness among workers is more explicit and overt than in the middle class.* The middle class, however, shows much labour political cohesion. In post-war elections the Labour Party has not succeeded in getting more than 20–25% of the non-manual vote or 10–15% of the business and professional classes. On the other hand at least a third of the working class consistently votes Conservative. Put another way, if (according to the 1961 Census) two-thirds of working population are employed in manual occupations, approximately one-half of the Conservative vote regularly comes from the working class, but only about one-sixth of the Labour vote from the middle class. (Figure IV.6). Indeed 'pure' class voting, or anything approaching it, would put an end to the British party system. The Conservative Party has survived the democratization of the country by its ability to gain votes of the poor. For that reason, the 'Tory working man' has been

*See below, p. 114.

FIGURE IV. 6: Sources of support for Parties, by class (N.O.P. 1964)

subjected to more study than the other politically deviant group, the middle-class Socialist. While some middle-class sympathy may be important to the Labour Party in providing it with leadership and local organization, and perhaps also in confirming its claim to speak for workers 'by hand or by brain', it does not have the statistical significance that working-class support has for the Conservatives.

What is the basis of working-class Toryism? The most important ingredient is social deference, though this may take many forms. In the nineteenth century Tory Democrats like Disraeli and Lord Randolph Churchill appealed to workers on the grounds that the Tories, unlike money-grubbing Liberal mill-owners, were true aristocrats and above the class-struggle. Factory hands who would not dream of voting for Mr Gradgrind could therefore confidently follow the Duke of Omnium. This appeal evoked, and still evokes, a response:

'The Conservatives have had more experience over the centuries. It's in the blood for them, running the country. There's more family background in the Conservatives, more of the aristocratic families, more heritage.

They're gentlemen born. I think they're made for that sort of job.'[17]

Coupled with it is a respect for education, remembering that education is at least as much social training as intellectual qualification: 'The Conservatives are better suited to running the country. They're better educated—I think there is nothing better than to hear a public school man speak English.'[18] But equally there is respect for money and business success—as indeed there was in the nineteenth century when a great many working men were willing to follow the lead of their local Liberal or Radical employers. Today money as well as birth is associated with Conservatism: 'The Conservatives do represent big business and I think that makes them the more efficient party. Running the country is, after all, just the biggest business of them all.'[19] To some extent the snobbish attitudes implied by this deference are reflected in the Tory worker's views of himself. Conservative manual workers are more likely to attribute middle-class status to themselves than Labour manual workers.[20] But deference implies just as strongly a desire to maintain the established distance between classes, to acknowledge the superiority of 'gentlemen born'.

Deference alone, however, can hardly account for the whole of working-class Conservatism. There is a second, less numerous, category, whom McKenzie and Silver call 'secular' Conservatives[21]— predominantly younger voters who happen to approve of private enterprise, value consumer affluence or view trade unions unfavourably.

They are less committed emotionally to leadership from the upper classes and take a more hard-headed and pragmatic view of Conservative capacity to govern. The fact that over the last twenty years the Conservatives have emerged relatively weaker in the older industrial areas (North of England, Scotland, Wales) than in the areas of more recent expansion (Midlands, South)* suggests that the secular element may be gaining over the traditionally deferential.

RELIGION, AGE, SEX, REGION

Class is so much the most important conditioner of political allegiance that it becomes difficult to disentangle it from others. There is overwhelming evidence that women are more conservatively inclined than men,[22] as in most other countries.[23] Men have given Labour a majority at every election since the war; women only in 1945 and 1966. If men only had voted, it is improbable that Dr Adenauer would ever have become Federal Chancellor of Western Germany, or that General de Gaulle would have been re-elected to the Presidency in 1965. Sex is the one factor which indubitably counter-balances class trends: working-class women are more right-wing than working-class men, middle-class women are more right-wing than middle class men. In certain Continental European states religion, especially Catholicism, plays an important part in making women more right-wing. In Britain, where this factor is less influential, the 'sex gap' is correspondingly smaller.

Age, too, correlates fairly closely with party preference, youth being more left-wing than middle age or old age.[24] Yet problems of causality arise. It may or may not be true that the older we get, the more conservative we become; in any case it has yet to be proved that this results in vote-switching on a large scale. It is also probably true that the older we get the higher we may rise in the social scale, though the opposite may also happen, and here some conscious switching of allegiance may well take place. At the same time the middle classes (who are known to be more conservative) have a higher expectation of life than the working classes, and women (who are also known to be more conservative) than men. Is the conservatism of the elderly a function of their age alone, or is it also a function of their class and sex?

The same difficulty confronts us over the influence of religion. There are valid historical reasons for associating the Church of England with Toryism, and Dissent (and Catholicism) with the Left. The Church of England is, after all, the Established Church; the alliance, at the national level, of Church and King, and at the local level of squire and parson, was bound to give it a Tory flavour. Macaulay called the

*See Figure iv. 8 below, p. 119.

Church of England 'the Tory party at prayer'. Dissenters, not merely because they were, until 1827, second-class citizens, but also because of the more democratic structure of their churches and the causes dear to the Nonconformist conscience, were drawn to Liberalism. Religious affiliation could indeed infect quite a stong ideological content into political loyalty. Mr A. J. P. Taylor, himself of Nonconformist origins, is quite confident of this:

'I doubt whether anyone with an Anglican background can become a true Radical. George Lansbury came nearest to it. Yet there was always a subtle dividing line between him and the rebels round him. Gladstone tried hard, but he could never rid himself of the belief that a duke or a bishop had more political sense than Cobden or John Stuart Mill. The rule still applies in the Labour Party. Its leaders with an Anglican education seek radical ideas, but they lack radical instincts . . . Religious dissent is the only safe background for a radical.'[25]

At the same time religion can fairly easily be equated with class and occupation. Here are lists of the most strongly dissenting English counties (a) in the 1850's (b) in the 1890's.[26]

1850's	1890's
Bedford	Bedford
Cheshire	
Cornwall	Cornwall
	Cumberland
Derby	Derby
Durham	Durham
Huntingdon	
	Isle of Ely
Lancashire	
Leicester	
Lincoln	
Monmouth	Monmouth
Northumberland	
	Nottingham
Stafford	Stafford
	Warwick
Yorkshire	Yorkshire (N & W ridings only)

Except for the 'Cromwellian' counties of Eastern England, these represent the country's principal mining and industrial areas. In political representation they were overwhelmingly Liberal. The outstanding change between the middle and the end of the century took place in Lancashire, where there was not only a successful Anglican counter-reformation but a marked swing to the Conservatives: between 1865 and 1906 the Liberals only once gained a majority of seats there.

One of the reasons for this swing to Church and Toryism was the influx of Irish immigration. The fact that from the beginning of the nineteenth century onwards most Catholics in Britain were either Irish labourers or their descendants naturally coloured Catholic politics. The Tories were the party of the Protestant ascendancy in Ireland, the Liberals the party of Home Rule. Catholics in Britain belonged overwhelmingly to the poorest classes. The question therefore is: does the predominantly left-wing affiliation of Nonconformists and Catholics simply reflect their social composition, or is there an independent, additional denominational factor? For the nineteenth century the evidence is incomplete. Almost all Dissenters active in politics were Liberals or Radicals and many of the leaders of Radicalism—Bright, Chamberlain, Lloyd George—were Dissenters. This may mean no more than that militant Dissent was overwhelmingly committed to Liberalism, though the example of Lancashire suggests that there was some correlation between denomination and party, transcending class. But it is worth remembering that even at the height of the Victorian religious revival, the urban masses remained largely untouched by religious observance, let alone sectarian disputes.[27] For the present day survey data are even more tenuous. It seems reasonably certain that the Liberals continue to enjoy disproportionately high support from Nonconformists,[28] but there is nothing to suggest that Labour, nationally, benefits from any residual dissenting radicalism (which has in any case declined in this century). In the areas of heaviest Irish immigration round Liverpool and Glasgow, sectarian feeling has tended to dominate politics and not only politics, as any spectator at a Celtic-Rangers match may observe. Here the Conservatives have emerged as the 'Orange' party, supported by Protestants of all classes. In Scotland generally, and in Glasgow particularly, working-class Catholics are much more strongly pro-Labour than working-class Protestants, and middle-class Catholics almost as strongly pro-Labour as Catholic workers.[29] Of Liverpool one American observer has remarked that it is the only English city he visited in which 'religious imprecations' heavily outnumbered the wall-slogans of CND and Fascists combined.[30] However, the exceptionally heavy swing to Labour on Clydeside and Merseyside over the past ten years suggests that even here sectarianism in politics is a declining force. For other parts of the country there are some indications to support the general impression that Catholics vote Labour more heavily* than their class structure would indicate,[31] but local samples are usually too small to be really reliable. The most interesting example of denominational politics which has been discovered in recent years is in Glossop, Derbyshire, *where among manual workers only*, members of the various churches voted as follows in 1951:[32]

	% Con.	% Lib.	% Lab.	% did not vote
Active Anglicans	55	5	29	12
Inactive Anglicans	43	5	36	15
Nonconformist	25	16	44	15
Roman Catholic	20	4	54	21
No religion	20	—	40	40

But Glossop is an old-established cotton town with highly traditional community ties; it may be more illustrative of popular, and largely out-of-date, stereotypes than of present-day reality.

There are similar difficulties in trying to isolate regional influences on voting behaviour. Scotland, Wales, East Anglia or Durham certainly have their distinctive voting characteristics. But is it really possible to distinguish the politics of coal, agriculture or shipbuilding from the sentiments of a region? In general, not. Durham is what it is because of coal, Clydeside because of ships, the Highlands because of crofting. But some regions are more distinctive than others. Distance from London or anti-English nationalism can play a part; so can religion, the only other factor capable of neutralizing the influence of class. This emerges most clearly in what is often referred to as the 'Celtic fringe'—Scotland, Wales and Cornwall. Its Anglican and monarchist connections have made the Tory Party predominantly English. It has failed to gain a majority of English seats in only four of the twenty-two elections since 1885: in 1906, 1929, 1945 and 1966, the years of its worst defeats. In Scotland, on the other hand, it has gained a majority of seats only five times, in 1900 (the first time ever), 1924, 1931, 1935, and 1955. In Wales the Tories have been in a minority since 1857; since 1885 they have only four times exceeded

---

*Professor Alford's discussion of the possible influence on Catholic voters of the Church's conservatism seems hardly relevant to Britain (*Party and Society*, pp. 139–41). Its connection with monarchical absolutism disappeared too long ago, and its link with the aristocracy is too tenuous, for this to count for very much. The same applies to the 'anti-Socialist political tendencies of the Church' (*ibid.*, p. 140). These are rooted in the experience of continental Europe, and arise out of the anti-clerical, rationalist and revolutionary character of the Liberal and Marxist movements. When a Catholic hierarchy was re-established in England after a lapse of 400 years, its first major intervention in social policy was in favour of the dock strikers in 1889.

a quarter of the seats (1895, 1924, 1931, 1935); once, in 1906, they held none at all.

Wales, therefore, presents the clearest examples of political regionalism in Britain. Its nationalism is radical and based on the chapel. Until 1918 this radicalism was expressed through the Liberal Party and found its greatest expression in David Lloyd George. The major constitutional grievance of Welsh Dissent was removed with the disestablishment of the Church in 1920. But the populist radicalism survived unweakened; Labour inherited its legacy not merely in the industrial South, where its natural social base was reinforced by the Depression, but in the rural areas also. Since the war the Liberals have lost five of their six remaining rural seats, all to the benefit of Labour. Only in Wales does Labour consistently hold non-industrial constituencies, such as Anglesey, Merioneth and Pembroke. Only in Wales do the Conservatives lose deposits not merely in the Rhondda, but in Carmarthen and Merioneth. Outside the coastal resorts, the border counties and the Cardiff area Conservatism is still regarded, as it was sixty years ago, as foreign, even hostile, to the interests and aspirations of Wales.

Popular radicalism was a much less important ingredient of Scottish Liberalism than of Welsh. Until well into the nineteenth century its leaders and parliamentary representatives were overwhelmingly aristocratic;[33] their social outlook was correspondingly more conservative. The hegemony of Scottish Liberalism came to an end in 1885 under the dual impact of the Third Reform Act (which emancipated the crofters) and the Irish Home Rule controversy. Significantly, the Conservatives in Scotland were until 1965 officially known as Unionists (i.e. favouring union with Ireland). But separatist feeling has kept Scottish Conservatism weak. Most of Labour's strength is derived from the industrial belt of Central Scotland, but of the remaining nineteen Border or Highland constituencies outside this belt the Conservatives held only eleven in 1966; five went to Liberals, three to Labour. As in Wales, the Liberal Party is associated with aspirations to self-government and is to that extent a rival to the self-confessedly nationalist parties. The association is, however, of long standing: it dates from the beginnings of the Church disestablishment controversies in the mid-nineteenth century and Liberal espousal of Irish Home Rule.

Regional political issues in Scotland and Wales are dominated by national sentiment. They do not solely arise, as they tend to in England, out of the problems of particular industries—for instance, the decline of heavy industry in the North-East in the early 1960's. The special rôle of the Liberal Party in expressing this Celtic discontent means that in rural Scotland and Wales there is three-party rather than two-party competition. The only area of England of which this is true is the South-West. Here, too, remoteness from London may be a factor; more relevant, probably, are the survival of a nineteenth-century social structure, the strength of Nonconformity, especially among farm-workers and small farmers, and the sparsity of large-scale industry. The four counties in which the contest is waged fairly equally between the three parties are Cornwall (the most strongly Celtic and dissenting of them) Devon, Dorset and Hereford.

Regional tradition may influence the long-term relative popularity of the parties in a given area; local community ties are much more important in shaping the individual's allegiances. Again, this is easiest to demonstrate for class-consciousness: the trend, not surprisingly, is to conform with the predominant character of the neighbourhood. The Newcastle-under-Lyme study showed that in the most heavily industrialized wards the proportion of manual workers who vote Labour is above the constituency's average, while in the farming and commuting areas it is below the average. It also emerged that only in the heavily working-class wards does Labour get appreciable support from non-manual workers.[34] The pressure of environment can influence not only party allegiance but the intensity with which it is felt. In 1950, when class-feeling ran more strongly than it does today, the group of seats with the highest median turn-out were those where Labour had majorities of over 40%. There were forty-eight such seats, thirty-three of them coal-mining, indicating 'a unique sense of working-class solidarity which has to be demonstrated at the polls'.[53]

The class basis of politics explains one of the minor curiosities of the British electoral system, namely a flaw in the 'cube law'. The cube law states that if the parties' votes are in the proportions of $A:B$, their seats in parliament will be in the proportions of $A^3:B^3$. Put differently, it means that a swing of 1% will cause between fifteen and twenty seats to change hands. Post-war elections have borne out the general validity of this law.

Swing and Seat changes, 1945–66

	Swing	Net gain in seats	Seats per 1% swing
1945–50	2·9	81	28*
1950–51	1·1	23	21
1951–55	1·8	24	13*
1955–59	1·1	21	19
1959–64	3·1	59	19
1964–66	2·7	46	17

*Indicates that there was a redistribution of seats.

However, on four occasions since the war (1950, 1951, 1955, 1959) there appeared a bias in the system in favour of the Conservatives of about $1\frac{1}{2}\%$—that is, to secure the same number of seats as the Conservatives, Labour would need about $1\frac{1}{2}\%$ (or 500,000 votes) more than the Conservatives. The reason for this lies in the uneven distribution of Labour support: Labour voters are mainly industrial workers and industry, especially heavy industry, tends to be concentrated in compact areas. Labour therefore 'wastes' more votes than the Conservatives. In 1951, when Labour won more votes, but fewer seats, than the Conservatives, thirty-seven out of forty-eight majorities over 20,000 were in Labour seats. In 1964 and 1966 this 'bias' disappeared. It might be tempting to attribute this to migration. The average electorate of Labour-held seats in 1966 was several thousands smaller than in Conservative-held seats. There is, however, no convincing evidence that Labour gained more seats *through migration alone* (i.e. through New Town or council estate development) than it lost (i.e. through middle-class commuter development). The main reason appears to be an above-average drop in the turn-out in safe Labour seats.* All that has happened is that Labour is under-polling about $1-1\frac{1}{2}\%$ of its potential support.

PARTY CHOICE

If it is true that social characteristics determine most people's party allegiance, what has happened to the concept of an election as choice? No two elections produce identical results. *Some* choice, therefore, does take place. Sociology in the main explains the reasons for long-term loyalty; psychology is more useful in explaining why some people change. Both emphasize the non-rational elements involved in political choice. A pioneer in this field was Graham Wallas, who in 1908 launched the much-abused term 'political image':

'The origin of a political party may be due to a deliberate intellectual process. It may be formed, as Burke said, by "a body of men united for promoting by their joint endeavours the national interest upon some particular principle in which they are all agreed". But when a party has once come into existence its fortunes depend upon facts of human nature of which deliberate thought is only one. It is primarily a name, which, like other names, calls up when it is heard or seen an "image" that shades imperceptibly into the voluntary realization of its meaning. As in other cases, emotional reactions can be set up by the name and its automatic mental associations. It is the business of the party managers to secure that these automatic associations shall be as clear

*See above, p. 88.

H

as possible, shall be shared by as large a number as possible, and shall call up as many and as strong emotions as possible.'[36]

One important variable is missing from this catalogue, however. The association needs not to be not only clear, widespread and strong, it must also be favourable. This is the most difficult one to guarantee, for the same image may stand the party in good stead one year and harm it in another. This applies, in particular, to a party's class image. The most important difference between Labour and Conservative supporters in their 'images' of the parties is that Labour people tend to see parties in terms of class interest or general aims ('for the working class', 'for the rich', 'for the man in the street'), while Conservatives do so in terms of issues or competence ('against nationalization', 'for individual freedom', 'having a clear policy').[37] This leaves wide open the question of how potent this image is under differing circumstances. The 'cloth-cap' image may well have helped Labour in 1945 or 1950; it was probably a liability by 1959, when memories of unemployment had faded and consumer affluence had eroded proletarian solidarity. The 'grouse-moor' image may well have helped the Conservatives in tapping the reserves of deference for most of this century; but in 1964 or 1966, when administrative failure and the leadership squabble had tarnished it, it became, temporarily at any rate, a vote-loser.

'Image' is also used, rather confusingly, to describe transient aspects of parties and political leaders which influence the mood of the moment. We may read that one man's 'television image' is unfavourable, perhaps because he has not mastered the techniques of the medium; or that a party's 'image' is one of disunity or lack of policies. Such factors change from one year to the next. They may well help to explain why people change their opinions, but they are not what Graham Wallas had in mind. His 'images' consisted of long-term attributes; their purpose is to establish a permanent brand-loyalty 'in the dim and shadowy region of emotional association'.[38] Image, as conceived by Wallas, is therefore more useful in explaining political loyalty than political change. There is, indeed, a good deal of evidence, both from this country and the United States, that many habitual supporters are either ignorant of their parties' programmes or in substantial disagreement with them. In one Bristol survey Conservative, Liberal and Labour voters scored respectively 60, 58 and 53% in attributing policy statements to the main parties: even completely random answers would have scored 50%.[39] Perception of issues is one matter, slavish adhesion to the party line is another. Party preference tends, after all, to be a relative rather than an absolute matter.

It is sufficient to agree with a majority of the party's stands on major issues, especially since some policy statements are themselves the outcome of bitter controversy within the party—one thinks of nationalization or defence in the Labour Party, decolonization or crime and punishment among Conservatives. Moreover, issues are not of equal importance. One person may be more concerned with the abolition of health service prescription charges, another with Rhodesia. Even so, the degree to which party policy is accepted is remarkably low and it tends to be lower among Labour than Conservative supporters. In Greenwich, for instance, the largest group of supporters within each party agreed with only 40–60% of official policies; 7% of Conservatives and 21% of Labour supporters were actually more in agreement with their opponents than with their own party.[40] Similarly the assessment of party leaders is not necessarily translated into electoral preference. In 1966, 55% thought that Mr. Wilson would make the better Prime Minister and 30% that Mr. Heath would.[41] But this 25% lead became a lead of only 6% in votes cast. All in all, the permanent image seems to be a more potent factor than changing issues or successive party leaders. It may even be more potent than rationally considered self-interest. After all, it by no means follows that the same party is at every election the best for the working (or middle) class, as most electors seem to think. There is a lot to be said for Professor Alford's view that it is 'class-based traditionalism', not ruthlessly evaluated economic interest, that is the chief motivator.[42]

Who, then, *does* change his mind? Is there such a creature as the 'floating voter'? It would probably be better if the term had never been invented. In the first place it must be remembered that the electorate itself is constantly changing. Every year approximately 600,000 adults die and 750,000 adolescents come of age. This alone could gradually affect the political balance in the country. But the word also suggests that the electorate can be conveniently divided into two categories, on the one hand the faithful supporter of the big battalions, on the other, earnest individuals seeking after truth. All survey evidence suggests the contrary: that there is a relatively small core of 'thick-and-thin men', shading off, through weak and conditional party-support into neutrality (or apathy). One survey, taken less than a fortnight before the 1966 General Election, illustrates this:[43]

How strongly would you say you support the Conservative/Labour/Liberal Party?

Very strongly	38%
quite strongly	36%
not very strongly	20%
not at all strongly	6%

How much do you personally care which party wins the
General Election?

Very much	40%
quite a lot	32%
not very much	22%
not at all	3%

These figures are very similar to those recently found in other
countries:

Intensity of Party Identification in USA,
Norway, and W. Germany (in per cent)[44]

	USA 1956	Norway 1957	W. Germany 1961
Strong identifiers	36	25	25
Weak identifiers	37	34	46
Independents (identification rejected)	23	25	5
Unpolitical (question not understood)	4	9	19
Not ascertained	—	7	5
	100	100	100

In fact, we can identify no fewer than four types of non-constant
electors—

1. those whose involvement with the party of their choice is
   low and who therefore hesitate between voting and abstention;
2. those who experiment with alternative allegiances but
   generally return to the party of their first choice at election
   time;
3. those who support a minor party but may be deprived of
   a candidate of their highest preference;
4. those who experience a genuine conversion and transfer
   their allegiance.

These four types between them amount to a substantial minority
among the electorate; and the total is certainly greater the number who
'float' in any one election. The contrast between the violent fluctuations of opinion polls and the relatively small swing at general elections
illustrate how much more numerous the potential waverers are than
the actual changers. Constituency surveys agree that anything up
to a quarter of electors have not firmly made up their minds at the

beginning of an election campaign.[45] Of course, the 'swing' figure
is misleadingly small. A 'net swing of 5% from Conservative to
Labour conceals reverse changes from Labour to Conservatives,
changes to and from both parties involving the Liberals, as well as
changes from abstention to voting and *vice versa*. Even so, the fact
that most waverers in the end revert to their former loyalties[46] is
significant, and confirms the existence of a gap between waverers and
actual changers.

Those who decide late and hesitatingly how they should vote could
be, and in traditional liberal mythology are, the independent-minded,
rational élite. Modern evidence, however, points overwhelmingly in
the opposite direction. In both Britain and America it has emerged
that 'waverers' are *on average* less well informed on current affairs,
less exposed to the political items in the newspapers or on radio or
TV, less likely to read election literature or attend meetings, less likely
to discuss politics with friends or members of their family.[47] The
pressures on them to participate in politics are either weaker than
for most other people, or they are contradictory. Electors subject to
'cross-pressures', e.g. whose family votes differently from most of their
friends or who are uncertain of their social status, have particular difficulty in making up their minds. The statistical evidence can deal in
averages only. Some of those who hesitate before voting almost certainly do live up to the liberal ideal of the rational citizen. But the
majority do not.

LOCAL ISSUES, PERSONALITIES AND BAND-WAGGONS

So far it has been assumed that all political choice in Britain is between
parties. The stability of party loyalties and the uniformity of the swing
show that this is indeed so. But local issues do arise and there are
frequent attempts to exploit them. It is remarkable how seldom this
works. Economic grievances are an obvious example of a potential
local issue. In 1959 parts of Lancashire and of Scotland swung to
Labour against the national trend, presumably because of the de-
pressed state of the cotton industry and shipbuilding, perhaps also
because of a general feeling that these areas were not sharing in the
growing affluence of the country. Conversely in 1964 the swing to
Labour in the West Midlands was below average, presumably because
the prosperity of that region gave less reason for discontent with the
Conservative Party. Regional deviations of this kind can be explained
in terms of spontaneous reaction by voters. Little or no persuasion is
needed by candidates or party leaders to bring them about. Moreover, the state of the economy looms so largely in most people's thinking about politics that it can hardly be isolated as a separate issue.

FIGURE IV. 7: Labour Party's share of major Party vote, 1966, by regions
(as defined by *The Economist*)

FIGURE IV. 8: Change in Labour Party's share of major Party vote
1945–66, by regions (as defined by *The Economist*)

Education and immigration are more promising as genuine local issues. In 1964 there was a below-average swing to Labour in the Bristol area and this was attributed to local opposition to the Labour council's comprehensive scheme; at any rate, Conservative candidates emphasized their sympathy with the opponents. Immigration was a more obvious, though by no means uniform, cause of deviant results in 1964. Swings to the right in Smethwick, Southall and Eton & Slough were obviously connected with resentment at coloured immigration, but other constituencies with equally heavy influxes (e.g. Brixton, Bradford E.) seemed less worried.[48] Anti-immigrant Independents in three constituencies secured between $7\frac{1}{2}$ and 10%, much the same as Sir Oswald Mosley had gained in 1959 in N. Kensington on a similar platform. But the rôle of the candidate is not the only factor. Mr Griffiths, who gained Smethwick from Labour, emphasized the issue; Sir Anthony Meyer, who gained Eton & Slough, admittedly on a much lower swing, did not. Local issues, it is evident, can influence individual results, but their impact is limited. Much more influential in encouraging or discouraging a propensity to swing is the social environment. Mining seats, where the class lines are more sharply drawn than anywhere else, have shown the lowest swings in either direction since the war. Predominantly rural seats, with their stable social relationships, have the next-lowest swings. As urbanization increases so does volatility, both in changes of opinion and in variations of turn-out.[49] The large cities show the greatest propensity to change, and the lowest turn-out of all. Urbanization may, therefore, affect our calculations of regional swings. Consistently low swings in East Anglia or the South-West are best attributed to the rural character of these areas; high swings in London or the North-West to their industrial character. Such factors cannot, however, account for long-term shifts in the political allegiance of different areas. Figure IV.8 shows that since 1945 the North and the older industrial areas have become markedly more favourable to Labour, the rest of the country (except Inner London) to the Conservatives.

Marginality also affects voting behaviour. Marginal seats did indeed show swings slightly above the average in 1964 and 1966, but there is no general tendency for them to contain a greater number of volatile electors. On the other hand, marginality has, since 1955 at any rate, helped to raise turn-out and to depress support for Liberal candidates.[50] This last point is important for any discussion of the function of parties in the British system, and the possible effects of electoral reform. We might expect the 'wasted vote' argument to weigh least in a marginal constituency, for two reasons. Marginal seats have, by definition, a more balanced social composition than safe ones (which are heavily middle-class or heavily working-class), and the Liberal party has the most evenly spread social following (see Fig. IV.6). Moreover a marginal seat offers the best opportunity for victory on a minority vote. Where the parties are evenly balanced a mere 35% may suffice to win a three-cornered fight. In fact, Liberals do exceptionally badly in marginal seats; we have already observed that the greatest Liberal successes have been in seats where the minority major party has no hope of success.* In Britain political success depends on the ability to form a strong government, and the elector in a marginal constituency is well placed to bestow or deny such success.

One further conclusion follows, namely that Liberal intervention has less effect on the outcome of a general election than is sometimes thought. Comparison between different types of contests enables us to calculate how Liberals would vote if they had no candidate of their own: [51]

1. In no election did the Liberals take more than 60% of their vote from one of the major parties.

2. Liberal voters are representative of the national trend. When the country is swinging right their votes are, in the majority, potentially Conservative (1950, 1951, 1955, less so in 1959); when the country is swinging left, their votes are, in the majority, potentially Labour (1945, 1964, uncertain in 1966).

3. In safe seats Liberal votes are drawn heavily from the minority party, in marginal seats much more evenly from both major parties, though with some regional variations.

Granted this, and the low Liberal vote in marginal seats, Liberals have had an important effect only twice since 1929. Had they contested no marginal seats in 1950, it is probable that the Conservatives would have become the strongest party, but without an absolute majority (instead of a Labour majority of five). Had they contested no marginal seats in 1964, Labour would probably have had a majority of ten, possible sixteen, instead of only four.[52]

If local issues count for little, what about the personality of the candidate? The *obiter dictum* of an anonymous election agent that 'no candidate is worth 500 votes'[53] has become part of British election mythology. Even if it were true it would not reduce the candidate to insignificance. In 1964 twenty-five seats were won by majorities of less than 500. Few personal characteristics of the candidate have any measurable impact on electors. Women fare no worse than men. Jews and Roman Catholics—with very few exceptions—fare no worse than Protestants. Those who stand on the Right of the Conservative Party or the Left of the Labour Party do no better and no worse than those who toe the line. There is, however, strong evidence that at least

*See above, p. 57-8.

two types of candidates do have a personal effect. The first consists of minor-party challengers. There is little doubt that most of the Liberals, members of other small parties and Independents who have succeeded in entering parliament since the war have done so, in part at least, on the strength of their personalities. The same applies to exceptionally good performances, especially at by-elections, which fell short of victory. Candidates of major parties can achieve less in this respect. All they can do is to build up a personal following on the basis of conscientious constituency service. This unquestionably does pay off, though there are pitfalls in calculating its exact extent. Different swings in seats defended by incumbents and newcomers could be due to regional bias or constituency-type bias (an excess of surburban over rural seats in the sample). Even taking this into account, it is evident that 'familiar' MPs may at the height of their popularity be worth extra swing of $1\frac{1}{2}$ to $3\frac{1}{2}\%$ to their party. This is an average: the exceptionally popular MP will be worth even more than that. There are two caveats, however. Very long-serving MPs may outstay their welcome and begin losing votes for their party. If, however, the MP concerned, like a wise prima donna, retires at the right moment, some of his increment stays with the party: his successor will suffer some loss of support, but not as much as a strict party average would indicate.[55]

The different behaviour of electors in marginal and safe seats, both in their decision whether to vote at all and in the support they give to minor parties, is evidence of increasing sophistication—a growing tendency to join in the social scientists' game of standing back and watching individuals reacting towards each other. There was, for instance, much greater interest in opinion polls in 1964 and 1966, if only because more organizations than ever before were making national and local predictions. All social science depends on the assumption that it is possible to make valid generalizations about human behaviour. All sampling techniques depend on the assumption that if a carefully chosen small percentage of individuals are studied, valid conclusions can be drawn about the whole of society. Opinion polls, and the publicity that surrounds them at election time, are subject to two criticisms. The first is that they are unreliable. This charge may be justly levelled at the majority of inexperienced organizations which dabble in this difficult exercise. Of the 54 individual constituency surveys conducted during the 1966 election eight had an error of more than 10% in their prediction of the final majority.[56] But the major polling businesses have been steadily improving their performance and they are unlikely ever again to commit mistakes like the notorious forecast of President Truman's defeat in 1948. The best records in 1966 were those of NOP and Research Services, using the random method, and Gallup, using the quota method*.

Accuracy of eve-of-poll forecasts, 1966[57]

	Actual result (GB only) %	NOP %	Gallup Quota %	Research Services %
Labour	48·7	50·6	49½	49·7
Conservative	41·4	41·6	41½	41·6
Liberal	8·6	7·4	8	7·4
Labour Lead	7·3	9·0	8·0	8·1
Error		1·7	0·7	0·8

A second criticism is that publication of the polls influences the outcome. People like to be on the winning side; the polls oblige by showing them which way the band-wagon is rolling. There is, however, no evidence that this is what happens, at any rate at General Elections. If the band-wagon effect had operated in 1966, Labour's lead should have increased in the course of the campaign, instead of decreasing as it in fact did. No doubt consistent prophecies of defeat depress the losing side who then anxiously search for scapegoats. No doubt a foregone conclusion robs a contest of much of its suspense and excitement. But to ban the publication of opinion polls—as has been suggested—would be a quite unjustified act of paternalism and would diminish even further the elector's right of free access to information.

Polls and sampling techniques are among the methods which have enabled us to know much more than even a generation ago how people vote, what conditions their allegiances, why they change their minds. There remains one further, vital, question: how relevant is the whole electoral process to government of a modern industrial state?

---

*The quota method requires the interviewer to collect interviews from persons he selects, provided their numbers are typical of the nation as a whole in age, sex and occupation. The random method requires him to interview respondents whose names have been randomly selected from the electoral register, leaving him no discretion. The eve-of-poll Gallup forecast, as published in The Daily Telegraph (March 31, 1966) was a combination of the quota survey and a less accurate random survey, giving a Labour lead of 11%—error: 3·7%.

REFERENCES

CHAPTER IV

1. Bryce, Viscount. *Modern Democracies* (London, 1921), pp. 168-9.
2. See Steed, M. in: Butler & King, *British General Election of 1964*, pp. 337-8; Berrington, H. B. 'The General Election of 1964' in *Journal of the Royal Statistical Society*, Series A, CXXVIII (1965), pp. 17-21; Rasmussen, J. S. 'The Disutility of the Swing Concept in British Psephology', *Parliamentary Affairs* XVIII (Autumn, 1965).
3. Jenkins, R. *Mr Balfour's Poodle. An Account of the Struggle Between the House of Lords and the Government of Mr Asquith* (London, 1954), pp. 202-8.
4. *Gallup Political Index* (monthly).
5. Figures kindly supplied by NOP.
6. Vincent, J. R. *The Formation of the Liberal Party, 1857-1868* (London, 1966), p. 17.
7. *Ibid.*, p. 81.
8. Stevenson, T. H. C. 'The Vital Statistics of Wealth and Poverty', *Journal of the Royal Statistical Society* XCI (1928), esp. pp. 211-2.
9. Durant, H. 'Voting Behaviour in Britain, 1945-64' in: Rose, R. (ed.) *Studies in British Politics. A Reader in Political Sociology* (London, 1966), p. 124. Supplementary information kindly supplied by Social Surveys (Gallup Poll) Ltd.
10. Hall, J. & Caradog Jones, D. 'Social Grading of Occupations', *British Journal of Sociology* I (March, 1950), pp. 33-4, 40.
11. Kahan, M., Butler, D. E. & Stokes, D. E. 'On the Analytical Division of Social Class', *British Journal of Sociology* XVII (June, 1966), p. 128.
12. *Ibid.*, pp. 128-9.
13. Alford, R. R. *Party and Society, The Anglo-American Democracies* (London, 1964), pp. 101-3.
14. Zölnhofer, W. 'Parteiidentifizierung in der Bundesrepublik und den Vereinigten Staaten' in: Scheuch, E. K. & Wildemann, R. (eds.), *Zur Soziologie der Wahl. Kölner Zeitschrift für Soziologie und Sozialpsychologie.* Sonderheft 9 (1965), p. 1953.
15. Rokkan. S. & Campbell, A. 'Citizen Participation in Political Life: Norway and the United States', *International Social Science Journal* XII (1960), p. 94.
16. Alford, *op. cit.*, p. 252.
17. Samuel, R. 'The Deference Voter', *New Left Review* I (January, 1960), p. 11.
18. *Ibid.*, *loc. cit.*
19. *Ibid.*, p. 12.
20. Runciman, W. G. *Relative Deprivation and Social Justice*, ch. IX; also Mark, Benney & Pear, *How People Vote*, p. 188; Bealey, Blondel & MacCann, *Constituency Politics. A Study of Newcastle-under-Lyme* (London, 1965), p. 176.

21. McKenzie, R. T. & Silver, A. 'Conservatism, Industrialism & the Working-Class Tory in England', *Transactions of the Fifth World Congress of Sociology* (1962); reprinted in Rose, *Studies in British Politics*, p. 28.
22. Durant, H. in Rose, *op. cit.*, p. 125; Butler & King, *British General Election of 1966*, p. 264.
23. Lipset, S. M. *Political Man* (London, 1960), p. 247.
24. Durant, H., *loc. cit.*
25. Taylor, A. J. P. 'The Thing', *The Twentieth Century*, October, 1957, p. 295.
26. Bealey, F. & Pelling, H. *Labour and Politics, 1900-1906*, pp. 3-4.
27. Inglis, K. S. *Churches and the Working Classes in Victorian England* (London, 1963), pp. 11-16, 329-30.
28. *Gallup Political Index B.9.* (March, 1966); Alford, *op. cit.*, p. 154-5.
29. Budge, I. S. & Urwin, D. S. *Scottish Political Behaviour. A Case Study in British Homogeneity* (London, 1966), pp. 63, 69-70.
30. Thayer, G. *The British Political Fringe. A Profile* (London, 1965), p. 236
31. Mark, Benney & Pear, *op. cit.*, p. 111; Campbell, P. W., Donnison, D. & Potter A. 'Voting Behaviour in Droylesden in October, 1951', *Manchester School of Economic and Social Studies* XX (January, 1952), pp. 62-3.
32. Birch, A. H. *Small Town Politics* (Oxford, 1959), p. 112.
33. Vincent, J. R., *op. cit.*, p. 48.
34. Bealey, Blondel & MacCann, *op. cit.*, pp. 182-3.
35. Nicholas, H. G. *The British General Election of 1950* (London, 1951), p. 318.
36. Wallas, G. *Human Nature in Politics* (London, 1908), pp. 83-4.
37. Bealey, Blondel & MacCann, *op. cit.*, pp. 206-13; Milne & Mackenzie, *Straight Fight*, pp. 131-40; Milne & Mackenzie, *Marginal Seat*, p. 129.
38. Wallas, *op. cit.*, p. 86.
39. Milne & Mackenzie, *Marginal Seat*, p. 121; Cf. Berelson, B. R., Lazarsfeld, P. F. & McPhee, W. N. *Voting. A Study of Opinion Formation in a Presidential Campaign* (Chicago, 1954), p. 230; Trenaman, D. & McQuail, J. *Television and the Political Image*, pp. 166, 215.
40. Mark, Benney & Pear, *op cit.*, pp. 145-6. Cf. Milne & Mackenzie, *Marginal Seat*, pp. 117-20; Birch, A. H., *op. cit.*, pp. 82-5; Donnison, D. & Plowman, D. E. G. 'The Functions of Local Labour Parties: Experiments in Research Methods', *Political Studies* II (February, 1954), pp. 162-4; Fienburgh, W. & others, 'Put Party Policy on the Agenda', *Fabian Journal* 6 (February, 1952), pp. 29-31; Berelson, Lazarsfeld & McPhee, *Voting*, pp. 223-7.
41. *The Sunday Telegraph*, March 27, 1966.
42. Alford, R. R., *op cit.*, p. 110, n. 13.
43. *Daily Mail*, March 24 1966.

44. American-Norwegian comparison: Campbell, A. & Valen, H. 'Party Identification in Norway and the United States', *Public Opinion Quarterly* XXV (Winter, 1961), p. 510; reprinted in: Campbell, A. & others, *Elections and the Political Order* (New York, 1966), p. 251. American-German comparison: Zölnhofer, W. in: Scheuch & Wildenmann, *op. cit.*, p. 113.

45. Milne & Mackenzie, *Marginal Seat*, pp. 36-8; Campbell, Donnison & Potter, 'Voting Behaviour in Droylesden', p. 61; Mark, Benney & Pear, *op. cit.*, p. 175.

46. Milne & Mackenzie, *Straight Fight*, pp. 130-1; Milne & Mackenzie, *Marginal Seat*, pp. 41-2.

47. Milne & Mackenzie, *Straight Fight*, pp. 96-8; Milne & Mackenzie, *Marginal Seat*, pp. 85, 103-4, 123, 154; Mark, Benney & Pear, *op. cit.*, pp. 176-8; Berelson & others, *Voting*, pp. 306-313; Lazarsfeld, P. F., Berelson, D. & Gaudet, H. *The People's Choice. How the Voter Makes up his Mind in a Presidential Campaign* (2nd edn., New York, 1948), p. 69.

48. Deakin, N. (ed.), *Colour and the British Electorate, 1964* (London, 1965), Chapters 2 and 7.

49. Butler & King, *British General Election of 1966*, pp. 279-80; Berrington, 'The General Election of 1964', pp. 23-9.

50. Butler & King, *op. cit.*, p. 285

51. Berrington, *op. cit.*, pp. 40-48.

52. Butler & King, *British General Election of 1964*, pp. 349-50.

53. Butler, D. E. *The British General Election of 1955*, p. 3.

54. Butler & King, *British General Election of 1964*, p. 353; *British General Election of 1966*, p. 287.

55. Williams, P. M. 'Two Notes on the British Electoral System', *Parliamentary Affairs* XX (Winter 1966-7), pp. 24-30.

56. *The Sunday Times*, April 3, 1966.

57. NOP: *Daily Mail*, March 31, 1966; Research Services: *The Observer*, March 27, 1966; Gallup: *The Daily Telegraph Gallup Analysis of the Election '66* (London, 1966), p. 140.

The Relevance of Elections

THE more we examine the electoral process at work under modern conditions, the more strongly we become aware of two main doubts about it. The first concerns its *efficacy*, the second its *relevance*.

IGNORANCE, IRRATIONALITY AND APATHY

Since elections are a device for expressing choice, we must assume that the participants are capable of making meaningful decisions. Before they can do this, they must have access to the necessary information, they must be willing to absorb it, they must be able to draw conclusions about it. On these counts, all the evidence so far discovered is discouraging. Few people are sufficiently interested in politics to follow or discuss current affairs regularly. Fewer still are accurately informed, or re-think their position in the light of this information from one election to the next. Those who do change their minds, and therefore decide alternations of power are, if anything, even less involved and worse informed than the regular 'ballot-fodder' of the main parties.

At first sight, this would seem to dispose of one of the classical arguments for universal suffrage, namely that most adults are the best judge of their own interests, and to lend weight to the emphasis of Graham Wallas and others on the irrational elements in political allegiance. To these objections, several answers may be given. In the first place, the argument from enlightened self-interest is not the only valid defence of universal suffrage. There is the argument of individual entitlement. No doubt the philosophical basis of the classical doctrine of natural rights, as it flourished in the seventeenth and eighteenth century, has taken some hard knocks; but perhaps the onus of proof is not on those who wish to include individuals within 'the pale of the constitution', but on those who wish to exclude them from it. It is by no means certain that the better-off or the better-educated are more rational and more disinterested in their political behaviour than those who left school at fifteen and earn their living by shovelling sand.

We should also be chary of jumping to conclusions about irrationality in electoral choice. To some extent it is a question of the standards we impose. The rational man, according to one authority,

'is open to new information, no matter whether it comforts or pains him. This means that he must actively seek information which is pertinent to the issues of the day, and it means that must not only seek that which is compatible with his own prejudices. [He] attempts to formulate an opinion on the basis of the best information available, selecting primarily on the basis of reliability and relevance.'[1]

Few of us would clear that hurdle without difficulty. What about the remainder? No doubt our values and attributes, of which political loyalties are a part, are often formed in early childhood by family or school environment. No doubt it is irrational to vote for a candidate because he is handsome or has kissed babies, or to support a party which promises to solve all problems by exterminating the Jews. But is it irrational to vote Labour out of class loyalties, or to vote as one's parish priest advises, if one considers him a well-qualified judge? As means to the desired end these are certainly rational. As for the ends themselves—a government favouring the workers, or a state based on Christian principles—our voters probably adhere to them for emotional and environmental, rather than coolly elaborated reasons. But it is dangerous to dismiss the values of others as unreasonable.

Above all it is a mistake to press the analogy between economic and political choice, as many of the classical Liberals were apt to do. The political market-place is different from the economic market-place. To buy one house rather than another, to prefer a refrigerator to a washing-machine, to invest in equities rather than gilt-edged are all individual and specific choices which require a fairly high degree of rationality. Failure to choose rationally results in measurable disadvantages. Prime Ministers, however, are not like houses and political parties are not like washing-machines. Our electoral choices are not specific, they are general. We choose between groups of politicians, some of whom have been familiar figures for years, perhaps decades. Or we choose between two party leaders on the basis of our broad impression of them. Unless we regard one issue or one sectional interest as overwhelmingly important, it is not much good tooth-combing the manifestoes. No doubt most politicians sincerely believe what they promise in the heat of a campaign. But we elect our rulers for five years at a time. Who knows what the balance of payments will be three years from now? Or what Central Africa may bring? Events which are difficult to foresee and impossible to control may make nonsense of the carefully laid schemes of the parties' pamphleteers. Detailed knowledge of policy statements, correct perception of party attitudes, clear understanding of individual speeches are no doubt admirable; but are they really necessary before an intelligent vote can be cast?

Just as the content and significance of voter ignorance and voter irrationality are often exaggerated, so are the content and significance of voter apathy. Meetings are poorly attended; canvassers and pollsters get luke-warm receptions; turn-out, especially in safe seats and at municipal elections, is often low and has been tending to get lower. What does this reveal about the health of British politics? In the first place it is easy to forget that most people are not very good at expressing themselves. Eager pollsters and fastidious analysts often mistake inarticulateness for ignorance or irrationality. Moreover, observers lump too many different states of mind together under the heading of 'apathy'. Strictly speaking, it should denote indifference. An apathetic person does not care, for reasons of ignorance, disillusionment or cynicism, who governs or by what policies. He has either deliberately opted out of involvement in public affairs in order to pursue some private objective, or considers it quite beyond his capacity to influence 'them' in any way. He is a-political. Apparently apathetic behaviour can, however, have a quite different explanation: it may reflect widespread acceptance of the way in which disputes are resolved. It may, therefore, be a symptom not of alienation or despair, but of homogeneity. If the political structure is in no immediate danger of being overthrown, if the general principles on which the political system is based are not in serious dispute, if the distribution of power between the major groups in society is unlikely to change rapidly or violently, if, therefore, political dispute is limited to ways and means of improving the existing structure—and this seems a fair description of the situation in most advanced, industrial nations—then there is not really very much to get excited about. Political controversy becomes limited, pragmatic and intermittent, rather than fundamental, ideological and endemic. The surface of political life is unruffled, hence the illusion of apathy.

High electoral participation, massive attendance at meetings, enthusiastic processions and heated discussions may, on the other hand, indicate fever, not robust good health. Between 1928 and 1932 participation in German parliamentary elections rose from 75% to 83%, while the Nazi party's share of the vote rose from $2\frac{1}{2}$% to 37%. Increased turn-out did not reflect greater civic consciousness, but panic. It represented the mobilization of the normally a-political (in the sense defined above) in the service of an exceptionally irrational and hysterical political appeal. In countries with stable parliamentary systems above-average turn-out may indeed be a response to a crucial

I

contest, e.g. in a marginal seat, but it can also indicate closely-knit inward-looking community ties, e.g. in coal-mining constituencies in Britain* or strongly Catholic villages on the continent of Europe. It then becomes an index of the internal homogeneity of a sub-group, not of that sub-group's integration into the national community.

The sudden mobilization of the a-political will almost certainly result in a violent upset of the normal balance of political forces, since the apathetic are, by definition, least strongly attached to traditionally established groups. But these are not the only conditions under which transient political formations may rise and fall in response to the circumstances of the moment. It was argued above that the prospect of violent or rapid change in the relative strengths of major groupings was important in determining the intensity of political strife. Indeed, it is probably the most important single factor, for general acceptance of the system, and consensus about political methods, must rest on the common assumption that cataclysmic changes are neither imminent nor desirable. Stability of this kind, however, is itself a consequence of political habits as well as their cause; it depends on how widespread and how strong is the electorate's sense of party identification. Where it is weak, as, for instace, in France,[2] party strengths, even for the short term, are much less predictable than in systems where strong party identification is widespread.

The stability of political loyalties, which is so marked in Britain, is therefore a source of strength to the British system of government. This might be dismissed as a platitude, but it is also a paradox. Party loyalty is, after all, rooted to some extent in obstinacy It rests on a reluctance to accept novel arguments or inconvenient facts, on a predilection for fitting thoughts into prearranged categories or stereotypes, on a temptation to judge arguments according to the source from which they emanate, on a readiness to rationalize or ignore inconsistencies. None of these characteristics contributes to rational thought as we have defined it. Yet at the same time stability of institutions discourages the search for oversimplified and extreme solutions, and the appeal to fears and prejudices in the mind of the voter. It is in seasons of chaos that the prophets of unreason flourish. If the twentieth century has taught us nothing else, it is that. The solution to the paradox lies in the intensity of party identification. Without strong—and therefore partly irrational—party loyalties, the system lacks foundations. But an organized interest can contribute to stability only if it recognizes the legitimacy of rival interests and their right to share in government. Party loyalty which is totally intransigent and self-

*See above, p. 112.

sufficient leads to a civil-war situation and the break-down of the system.

If British experience is at all significant, then lack of information, poor perception of issues, and allegiances which have at best a partially rational basis are not fatal to the workings of a representative system. The implications of this are raised in the pioneering American study of electoral behaviour, *Voting:*

'If the democratic system depended solely on the qualifications of the individual voter, then it seems remarkable that democracies have survived through the centuries ...

Individual voters to-day seem unable to satisfy the requirements for a democratic system outlined by political theorists. But the system of democracy does meet certain requirements for a going political organization. The individual members may not meet all the standards, but the whole nevertheless survives and grows. This suggests that where classic theory is defective is in its concentration on the individual citizen.'[3]

A theory fitting the known contemporary facts would therefore place less emphasis on institutions or individual psychology, and more on the political culture of a society. To help in balancing conflict against stability a distribution of labour, between the enthusiasts and the passively committed, may be useful. Common sense and inherited habits can operate as substitutes for individual rationality, since political choice is, at best, crudely defined and broadly delineated. Conclusions such as these must be tentative; the hypothesis that a certain amount of apathy contributes to political equilibrium within a society has its attractions, but it has yet to be proved beyond dispute. According to its critics, it rests on 'arguments ... too loose to convince and too complacent to excite'.[4] Even if valid, it does not supersede the case for better civic education or the reform of institutions. But it does help to emphasize the habits of mind, which cannot be quickly or easily changed, are an important—perhaps decisive—*datum.*

MAJORITIES AND MANDATES

During the eighteenth and nineteenth centuries many Conservatives and Liberals opposed the indiscriminate extension of the suffrage because they feared that the majority of electors were not fitted, intellectually or morally, for the exercise of this right; and that if they were allowed to exercise it without restraint the result would be an end to individual liberty and the rights of property.

'In a democracy [wrote James Madison] where a multitude of persons exercise in person the legislative functions, and are continually exposed, by their incapacity for regular deliberation and concerted measures, to the ambitious intrigues of their executive magistrates, tyranny may well be apprehended, on some favourable emergency, to start up in that quarter.'[5]

His contemporary, Thomas Jefferson, warned:

'It will be no alleviation, that these powers will be exercised by a plurality of hands, and not by a single one. One hundred and seventy-three despots would surely be as oppressive as one . . . As little will it avail us that they are chosen by ourselves. An *elective despotism* was not the government we fought for . . .'

John Stuart Mill, eighty years later, inveighed against 'a government of privilege, in favour of the numerical majority, who alone possess practically any voice in the State'.[7]

Modern research into electoral behaviour has tended to support the pessimists' premises more strongly than their conclusion. We have seen that the political climate of a society can counter-balance the short-comings of institutions or individual voters. But it can do so on one condition: the political system will remain stable only if the main contending forces within it are unable to deal each other knock-out blows, and if the main contestants are confident that this is so. Mill foresaw a different contingency:

'In all countries there is a majority of poor, a minority who, in contradistinction, may be called rich. Between these classes, on many questions, there is complete opposite of apparent interest . . . Is there not a considerable danger lest [the majority] should throw upon the larger incomes, an unfair share, or even the whole, of the burden of taxation; and having done so, add to the amount without scruple, expending the proceeds in modes supposed to conduce to the profit and advantage of the labouring class?'[8]

An ultra-Conservative might be tempted to argue that sur tax and the welfare state have borne out Mill's darkest fears; but it can hardly be seriously maintained that all states with universal suffrage have been governed consistently and exclusively for the benefit of wage-earners and 'the poor'. Society is more complex than Mill (or Marx) imagined, and the evolution of industry has made it more, not less, complex. Political loyalties have other sources beside self-interest, correctly or incorrectly perceived. Both sides in the classical debate about Radicalism and Democracy arrived at the wrong answer, because both asked the same, wrong question. Neither the sovereignty of the people, nor the tyranny of the majority, as conceived of a hundred or a hundred and fifty years ago, has come to pass, for if we examine 'the people' and 'the majority' under a microscope we discover that they disintegrate into their component parts.

Concepts like 'the will of the people', and 'majority rule' make political sense only on the assumption that the people or the majority can, through elections, translate their interests into public policy. If they cannot, then the hopes of Tom Paine or Richard Roebuck will be disappointed, and the fears of James Madison and John Stuart Mill be proved groundless. We therefore have to ask: how effective are elections as determinants of policy? The evidence presented in Chapter IV points against their effectiveness. Most electors, it emerged, vote in accordance with habit rather than the immediate issues at stake (though the one does not, of course, exclude the other); not many electors have clear knowledge of the issues stressed by the candidates; fewer still can identify the parties' stands correctly; a significant number wittingly or unwittingly vote contrary to their policy preferences.

No election in Britain is ever fought on a single, overwhelmingly important issue. No party and no major-party candidate ever campaigns on one issue only. The reasons for this are three-fold. A British election centres principally on the capacity of the parties to provide effective government over a broad range of topics. Secondly, each of the major parties is trying to appeal to a majority of the electorate, including some who have in the past voted, or might vote, for the other party. It is hardly likely that the same coherent, ideologically consistent, policy statement will appeal with equal strength to all potential supporters. Teachers may want to compare the parties' educational policies, retired people their pensions policies, house-buyers their mortgage policies. But not all teachers, retired persons or house-buyers will give their own sectional considerations priority—anyway a person may be both a teacher and a house-buyer—and they will certainly not all interpret the programmes offered them in the same way. Thirdly, the parties themselves, especially in a two-party system, are coalitions of disparate interests. These interests accept each others' claims in order to be able to press their own, and to secure a share in the benefits that a parliamentary majority can bestow. There is no logical connecting link between the Labour Party's support for the nationalization of steel, the enfranchisement of leaseholds and state aid to Church schools. Each majority that emerges from an election, therefore, turns out not to be a coherent expression of the people's voice, but a successful coalition of groups with differing priorities. This is what Prof Dahl has named 'minorities rule'.[9]

'In no large nation-state [he continues] can elections tell us much about the preferences of majorities and minorities, beyond the bare fact that among those who went to the polls a majority ... or minority indicated their first choices for some particular candidate or group of candidates. What the first choices of this electoral majority are, beyond that for the particular candidates, it is almost impossible to say with much confidence ...

If the majority rarely rules on matters of specific policy, nevertheless the specific policies selected by a process of 'minorities rule' probably lie most of the time within the bounds of consensus set by the important values of the politically active members of the society.'[10]

This hypothesis, while denying that parliamentary elections are a satisfactory way of determining specific questions of policy, leaves open the wider question of whether most voters are swayed by specific policy issues at all.* Even this is, however, doubtful. Single issues are more likely to predominate in local than in national elections: an interesting test case of this was the election for governor of Wisconsin, USA, in 1962 which was fought on the issue of a sales tax (supported by the Republican candidate) *versus* higher income tax (supported by the Democrat) and narrowly won by the Democrat. Of voters interviewed, only a quarter claimed that they made their choice primarily on the tax issue. Of these a majority voted for the victorious Democrat; those who switched to him from their normal allegiance were more numerous than normal Democrats who switched to his opponent. Here, it might appear, is an undoubted mandate for higher income taxes. But is this really justified? Against those who voted Democratic solely because of the tax issue must be put the much larger number who voted for the Democrat, simply because he was the Democrat. Indeed, those who voted for him *although they preferred the sales tax* considerably outnumbered the pro-income tax switchers.[11]

If modern representative democracy has any theoretical foundation at all, then it is in the proposition that the wish of the numerical majority should prevail. The majority of Wisconsin voters preferred the Democratic candidate and he was duly elected. But those who preferred him primarily for tax reasons amounted to only 28% of his own supporters and 14% of the total voters. This episode from the Mid-West is of relevance to a question often raised in British con-

*At one point Dahl implies that they are (*A Preface to Democratic Theory*, p. 128).

stitutional discussion: Does victory in a general election bestow a mandate on those who win it?

The idea of using general elections as plebiscites, or 'appeals to the people' is an old one; certainly the dissolution of 1784 was an attempt to gain a majority for Pitt, whom George III had just appointed Prime Minister. But any time before 1832 such an appeal was less to 'the people' than, as Creevey noted, to the Treasury,[12] and never more so than in the (successful) appeal of 1784.[13] The election of 1831 was fought for or against parliamentary reform, and the overwhelming Whig victory ensured that reform would pass. But it is only since the reform of 1832 that there has been any traceable relationship between the state of public opinion and the composition of the House of Commons; and only since then, therefore, that the theory of the mandate has been at all plausible. Other elections since 1832 have been fought, at any rate in the eyes of the contestants, on specific issues: that of 1886 on Irish Home Rule, that of 1906 on free trade, those of 1910 on the powers of the House of Lords. There is no doubt that had these elections resulted differently this would have affected the policies to be pursued: the parties which won and those which lost had both declared in advance what they would do if elected. What we do not know is how many voters were swayed by the dominant issue.

That, however, is the least of the difficulties which such a theory of the mandate raises. We need also to ask: does the mandate extend equally to all items of a party's programme? The Labour Party is committed to steel nationalization and has twice, in 1948 and 1965, attempted to carry this policy into effect. It can no doubt claim that anyone who voted Labour knew—or could easily have found out—that steel nationalization would be a natural consequence of a Labour victory. But it cannot be demonstrated whether Labour voters supported this policy explicitly or merely by implication.

The doctrine of the mandate is clearly more attractive to Radicals and Socialists, who believe that parliament exists to carry out the instructions of the electors, than to Liberals or Conservatives, who lay greater emphasis on the independent judgment of Parliament. The Radical view, however, raises a second difficulty: if a government is under an obligation to carry out its mandate, is it also entitled to exceed it? A great many of the most important decisions by British governments have been introduced without prior leave by the electorate. This is true of the repeal of the Corn Laws in 1846, of Gladstone's first Irish Home Rule Bill in 1886, of the Liberal government's social legislation between 1906 and 1910, of the National Government's introduction of a tariff in 1932, of Mr Macmillan's decision to apply for British membership of the Common Market in 1961. It is on occasions such as these that the doctrine of the mandate becomes attractive to conservatives, for it can then be argued that innovations should await the approval of the electorate. This was the argument used by the Marquess of Salisbury in opposing the abolition of the death penalty, which the Commons had voted to do, in 1956:

'This question of capital punishment has quite definitely not been put before the electorate at the last or, so far as I know, any other General Election. I know, of course, that there are, on occasions, questions, it may be great questions, which blow up suddenly between elections, and on which the electorate cannot, in the nature of things, be consulted ...

But this question of the abolition of the death penalty is no sudden issue, utterly unforeseen, which could not possibly have been raised at the General Election ... I had the curiosity to inquire what mention of capital punishment there had been in the Election addresses of those Members in all parties who have supported this Bill in the House of Commons. What did I find? Not a single one had ever mentioned the subject in his Election address ...

It seems to me quite impossible for Parliament in this country to pay lip-service to democracy in theory and not to accept its implications in practice. To say that we trust the people when the people happen to agree with us, and to fail to trust the people in practice, when the people happen to take a rather different view—that way, to my mind, lies the destruction of free democracy.[14]

Lord Salisbury is entitled to blame abolitionist MPs for their lack of candour on a topic which they judged to be a vote-loser; but he gets no nearer than any other advocate of the mandate theory to explaining how the electorate's views on this topic could be singled out from their views on any other in the course of a General Election. Nor does an episode from the 1966 election get us much further. An Independent candidate who favoured the retention of hanging stood against Mr Sydney Silverman, the Labour promoter of the abolitionist bill. He got 13.7% of the vote, which appeared to be drawn almost equally from Mr Silverman and his Conservative opponent. This demonstrated that 13.7% of the voters in that constituency (Nelson & Colne) felt sufficiently strongly on the issue to desert their normal allegiance. We do not know for certain how they would have voted in the absence of an Independent; nor do we know the views on hanging of the 83.6% who voted Labour or Conservative, or of the 49.3% who voted for the country's chief abolitionist legislator. Similarly, Lord Salisbury's thesis sheds no light on the third major difficulty: how far a government may take policy initiatives on topics which, though of great national importance do not arise overnight. An outstanding example is the

dispute over re-armament in the 1930's. Against Stanley Baldwin's
defence that the government had had no mandate for such a step,
Churchill insisted that 'the responsibility of ministers for the public
safety is absolute and requires no mandate'.[15] Events justified him. In
April, 1939, Baldwin's successor, Neville Chamberlain, announced
peace-time conscription, without a mandate.

THE VOTER'S CHOICE

The emphasis on the individual voter's inadequacy for his responsi-
bilities is one frequently-voiced criticism of the electoral process. But
the voter, too, has his complaints, as he perceives how little influence
he has on the way he is governed. This is not merely an argument
about the mandate theory, about whether or not the system allows the
voter to answer specific questions. The complaint goes deeper than
this: that the questions which voters are asked are not necessarily the
ones they wish to answer. They choose between two or three candidates in the constituency, but have little influence in their nomination.
They choose between Mr Heath and Mr Wilson, or between Mr
Macmillan and Mr Gaitskell, but they were never asked whether they
wanted any of these men to be the chief aspirants to the Premiership.
On some issues the parties have opposed views; on others not. Both
major parties are committed (for instance) to the Atlantic alliance, to
compulsory education, to the basic principles of the welfare state, to
the maintenance of full employment. The voter who wants a neutralist
or pro-Soviet foreign policy, voluntary education or two million un-
employed has little chance of casting an effective vote if he wants his
views represented.

These are severe limitations on the individual's political power. In
part, they illustrate a problem common to all advanced, industrial
nations, Eastern or Western. The gap between those who take the
decisions and those who have to carry them out is becoming wider
everywhere, partly because of the growing centralization of power,
whether political or economic, but also because of the increasing
reliance on 'technocrats' who command skills which the ordinary man
does not understand. The distance between the citizen—however generously the constitution may define his rights—and the real sources
of power appears to be getting greater and greater all the time. More
and more power seems to be concentrated in the hands of the bureau-
crat, the manager, the party boss, the trade union leader. Various
remedies have been proposed—regional devolution, workers' control
in industry, community projects, 'participatory democracy'—all designed to bring the individual into more effective contact with the decisions that concern him. The contemporary protest movements—
CND in Britain, civil rights in America—have their roots in the belief

that existing parliamentary institutions are useless for bringing about major policy changes. Though the problem is an international one, there is a peculiarly British dimension to it. British democracy is highly élitist, more so than that of many other states wth parliamentary systems. Britain has never known the referendum, the popular initiative, the nominating convention, the primary or the write-in vote, and the prospects of any of these devices being introduced here seem remote. Not merely the British social structure but the whole evolution of our representative institutions explain why there are so few checks on the behaviour of elected legislators. What has happened is that Parliament, feudal and patrician in origin, has adapted itself to the widening of civil liberties and the extension of the right to vote. Certainly, most of the decisive changes happened under the impulse of popular radicalism. But none has been achieved by revolution, and in the absence of a British revolutionary tradition the slogans and symbols of popular sovereignty, so important in America or France, carry little weight.

Joseph Schumpeter's thesis that democratic elections amount to no more than competition between élites is therefore particularly applicable to Britain:

'In political life there is always some competition, though perhaps only a potential one, for the allegiance of the people. To simplify matters we have restricted the kind of competition for leadership which is to define democracy, to free competition for a free vote. The justification for this is that democracy seems to imply a recognized method by which to conduct the competitive struggle . . .

Between [the] ideal case which does not exist, and the cases in which all competition with the established leader is prevented by force, there is a continuous range of variation within which the democratic method of government shades off into the autocratic by imperceptible steps . . .'[16]

Arguing that the true function of the electorate's vote is the acceptance of leadership, he concludes, 'The principle of democracy then merely means that the reins of government should be handed to those who command more support than to any of the competing individuals or teams.'[17] This is a substantial modification of Aristotle's definition: we no longer have 'the sovereignty of the majority', but the consent of the majority. Free elections in Britain mean free choice between policies and leaders, but little freedom in establishing the terms of the choice. When it comes to the drawing up of party policy and the selection of party leaders, the élitist character of British politics emerges strongly.

The methods by which policy is formulated have always been more controversial in the Labour Party than among Conservatives and Liberals, for reasons which have already been discussed.* Writing in 1937, shortly after he had become Leader of the Labour Party, Attlee defined the rôle of the party's annual conference as 'a parliament of the movement':

'In contradistinction to Conservative conferences which simply pass resolutions that may or may not be acted upon, the Labour Party Conference lays down the policy of the Party, and issues instructions which must be carried out by the Executive, the affiliated organizations, and its representatives in Parliament and on local authorities.'[18]

This is not quite how Attlee managed the Labour Government of 1945–51, of which he was Prime Minister; 'You can't', he recalled afterwards, 'have a non-parliamentary body arranging things, saying "You must do this. You mustn't do the other" '.[19] Nor was it an accurate description of the situation in 1937, for the Labour Party had already then been in office twice, and the conflict between a government's responsibility to parliament or the party outside was not a new one. The way in which Ramsay MacDonald had formed and conducted the first Labour Government in 1924 showed that the Labour Party was as fully part of the established parliamentary system as the Conservative and Liberal Parties, and subsequent attempts to reassert the sovereignty of conference failed. 'I am not going to have ropes around my neck for other people to pull when they like,' MacDonald announced.[20] Indeed the Parliamentary Labour Party has tried, almost from its beginnings in 1906, to emancipate itself from (in Keir Hardie's words) 'definite instructions to introduce this and that'.[21]

It is sometimes argued that the power of the Labour Party Conference varies according to whether the party is in opposition or power. According to this view it is legitimate for the conference to lay down future policy committments, as it did in 1945, when it itemized the industries to be nationalized, against the wishes of the National Executive Committee; it is not legitimate to dictate policy to H. M. Ministers. This is an unreal distinction. What is the use of recommending policies, if you cannot control those in whose hands lies the decision whether to carry them out when they are in power?

*See above, p. 62–4.

The question of who controls whom in the Labour Party has been debated many times, and it was probably decided conclusively in 1960–61 in the course of the debate on nuclear weapons. In 1960, at Scarborough, the conference reversed official party policy and backed unilateral nuclear disarmament, while the majority of Labour MPs did not. Hugh Gaitskell, in his speech at that conference, asked delegates how they envisaged the situation of MPs who disagreed with the conference decision on so fundamental a matter.

'What do you expect of them? You know how they voted in June—overwhelmingly for the policy statement . . . So what do you expect them to do? Change their minds overnight? To go back on the pledges they gave to the people who elected them from their constituencies? And supposing they did do that? Supposing all of us, like well-behaved sheep, were to follow the policies of unilateralism and neutralism, what kind of impression would that make upon the British people?'[22]

It was not merely a scholastic interpretation of the Labour Party's constitution that was involved here; the basic question was one which lies at the centre of all representative systems—is the elected legislator a delegate, and, if so, whose? Since, in the following year at Blackpool, the Conference reversed its 1960 decision and fell into line with official policy, the outcome of this particular dispute was a clear victory for the parliamentary party and Mr Gaitskell.

In the Liberal and Conservative parties the rights of conference delegates have provoked less controversy. Ever since the newly-formed extra-parliamentary bodies overplayed their hands in the 1880's and 1890's, the parliamentary leadership has been firmly in charge, irrespective of whether it was in power or in opposition. There have, of course, been critical debates at Conservative conferences: that of 1903 on tariff reform, that of 1921 on the Treaty with the Irish Free State, that of 1934 on Baldwin's India policy, and that of 1962 on the Common Market. In 1934 the official policy survived by only 543 votes to 520;[23] but as a rule the challenge to the platform is feeble—so feeble that the chairman of the 1962 conference could commit the Freudian slip of announcing, 'We will take the [hostile] amendment first, and after that has been beaten we will vote on the main question'.[24]

The *de facto* primacy of the parliamentary leaders over the party conferences has its limits. True, the rank-and-file cannot *instruct* the leaders, especially when these are also government ministers. But it is not true (as Michels claims it is) 'that the history of parliamentary parties consists of a succession of rejected congress decisions'.[25] Party leaders cannot afford to be frequently disavowed by their own followers, and the appearance of disunity is always bad for the party's public image. For this reason the rebels in the Labour Party during the 1950's saw with some satisfaction that official policy was often trimmed to anticipate their objections. And if the 1961 Labour conference had reaffirmed the 1960 decision in favour of unilateralism it would have been politically, even if not constitutionally, necessary for Mr Gaitskell to resign the leadership—something which he had himself privately acknowledged.[26]

While the internal politics of the Labour Party centre on policy disputes, in the Conservative Party the manner of choosing the leader is the main source of conflict. Just as Labour has in these matters inherited the radical-democratic tradition, and turns instinctively to election as the normal method, so the Conservatives have acted, as far as they could, in accordance with the hierarchic principle. The mystical qualities with which the leadership is thereby endowed emerge in the famous declaration by Capt. Pretyman, MP, in 1923: 'Great leaders of parties are not elected, they are evolved ... The leader is there, and we all know it when he is there'.[27] There was not a democratic method and it was not meant to be, and for this reason was criticized not only by anti-Conservatives but by reformers within the party. It could not survive the leadership crisis of 1963, when Sir Alec Douglas-Home was chosen to succeed Mr Macmillan, and when, although justice may have been done, it was not seen to have been done. As a result the leader of the Conservative Party, like the leaders of the Labour and Liberal parties, is now elected by his party's members in the House of Commons, Mr Heath succeeded Sir Alec Douglas-Home in this way in 1965.

Who makes policy and who chooses the leader are important questions in determining the degree of intra-party democracy. But whatever the answer the ordinary voter may remain dissatisfied. Whether the leader of the Conservative Party is to be nominated by what Mr Macleod christened 'the magic circle'[28] or by a few hundred MPs is a debate within the élite about the extent of the élite. So is the debate whether party policy should be drawn up with or without the aid of party militants. All that can be said is that the more extensive the élite, the more sensitive it becomes to indirect pressures from outsiders. Back-bench MPs can be lobbied in a way that Chief Whips cannot; conference delegates are, for the rest of the year, friends and neighbours in a way that Cabinet Ministers (or shadow ministers) are not. It may not be just, but it is surely unavoidable, that those citizens who are politically active have more influence than those who are not; public opinion, after all, consists of 'those opinions held by private persons which governments find it prudent to heed'.[29]

THE RELEVANCE OF ELECTORAL CHOICE

The contemporary British voter who asks himself what say he has in his country's affairs must be assailed with one further doubt. He may agree that he has little chance as an individual of influencing election manifestoes or the choice of leaders; but what of the parliament and the cabinet which emerge from the election? How many of the really important policy decisions do they make? How many of the effective choices are theirs? Who runs Britain? And is it in the first place the elected parliamentarians who do so?

Marxists have always had a ready-made answer to these questions. Real power lies in the hands of those who own the means of production. When their interests are at stake they are always in a position to exert pressure—on MPs, ministers, civil servants or mass media—to ensure a decision in their favour. Electoral competition is therefore a façade, parliamentary debate a farce. It would be difficult to maintain, in the face of the evidence, that all parliamentary politics in the past hundred years has been merely a capitalist racket. But even if this were agreed, it would not answer the further question, namely, where and by whom are the crucial decisions made?

In the course of this century the concept of the self-regulating market in matters of wages and prices has been left further and further behind. Wage negotiations now take place on an industry-wide basis, between representative organizations which enjoy official standing and may be subject to some public scrutiny. In many professions, the standard of qualifications and of conduct is determined by private, monopolistic bodies—the Inns of Court, for instance, or the British Medical Association. Professor Gunnar Myrdal's verdict on these velopments is typical of many:

'If it sometimes looks as if the state had left it to the powerful organizations themselves to fight it out and come to an agreement ... this is only so because it is felt that the balance of strength between the buyers and the sellers in the market has been established by state intervention. These organizations then actually function as organs for public policy ...

Many of the most important decisions, then, are taken outside parliament, and put into effect by other organs than those of the state administration.'[30]

A ten per cent wage increase in the engineering industry, or a railway strike, may have more impact on the country's affairs than the whole of one year's legislation. Even when the state is involved with the private partners, its rôle may be only passive and subordinate. Although manufacturing industries or agriculture may depend on the state for protective tariffs, fixed prices and subsidies they can, if they are sufficiently well organized, often dictate their own terms.

Because there is a general tendency for producer groups—whether of goods or of professional services—to organize in defence of their interests, and because modern governments increasingly depend on such groups for information or expert advice, the biggest lobbies have come to assume important representative functions. Professor Beer is convinced that

'producer groups have a power to affect policy-making that is quite separate from their position in the system of parliamentary representation and party government...

The source of the power is not the fact that the group or its members has (sic) a rôle—for instance, as voters or contributors to party funds—in the system of parliamentary representation, but derives from the group's performance of a productive function.'[31]

In the nineteen-fifties this could lead to a sort of corporative stagnation, where progress was possible 'with near unanimity, or not at all'.[32] Despite the two-party system, therefore, which is supposed to lead to strong governmental leadership, Britain seemed to be immobilized by a multi-party coalition of economic interests, operating by the side of, and through, the state machine. If the economic power of the producer groups were such that they could permanently impose their wishes on both parliament and the civil service, then the voter would certainly be entitled to wonder what his contribution was worth. But if Beer is right, and the groups' power drives precisely from their integration into the modern 'mixed', 'managed' or 'planned' economy, there is no inherent reason why the state should continue in this passive rôle.

Indeed, in this respect the situation has radically changed since the mid-fifties. With the setting up of the National Economic Development Council (NEDC or Neddy) in 1962 and the Prices and Incomes Board (PIB) in 1965 the government took a decisive step towards a more positive rôle, to indicative planning as opposed to holding the ring. Beer is therefore looking at NEDC through the spectacles of the 1950's in describing it as an 'agency of functional representation';[33] the government's declared intention of maintaining a permanent watching brief* on wages, prices and incomes, quite apart from such temporary measures as the 'freeze' or the 'period of severe restraint' (1966–67) restores to the politician a degree of initiative which is bound to revise our view of the relevance of elections. The greater the power of the organized groups *vis-à-vis* the state, the more the individual must look to these groups as his most effective representatives. The greater the power of the state *vis-à-vis* the organized groups, the more the voter comes into his own.

As a result, expectations, or experience, of the partes' attitudes to different groups becomes an important factor in electoral choice. Will a particular minister be tough with the trade unions, lenient with the farmers, conciliatory towards the doctors, unbending towards ship-building or the aircraft industry? Such issues can become electorally relevant. They are, no doubt, far removed from the legislative func-tion of parliament, as traditionally conceived; but if, by procedural reforms and an extension of the committee system, Members of Parlia-ment are to share increasingly in the making of national policy, this could transfer even more power to those who are, in the last resort, answerable to the electors and amenable to public complaints.

HOW REPRESENTATIVE? HOW DEMOCRATIC?

Was Rousseau right after all? Are the British people free only once every five years? There have, no doubt, been times when the actions of the government, and of parliament, have gone clearly against the wishes of the public; or when the public have had only inadequate or mis-leading information on which to judge these actions; or when well-organized minorities have been able to nobble the agencies of the state at the expense of the interests of the majority. But exactly how great is the distance between the individual citizen and the well-springs of power? Exactly how difficult is it for the majority to express and impose their wishes?

In any system of elective representation the rights of the indi-vidual voter are of necessity exercised indirectly, not merely because most political communities are too large for the primitive forms of

*Cf. the speech by the Chancellor of the Exchequer, Mr L. J. Callaghan, at the Labour Party Conference of 1966: 'Any group of people who are arguing about their incomes, whether it is workers about their wages or landlords about their rents, must accept and recognize that the bargaining strengths of the two parties is not the only factor that can be allowed to decide these issues in future.

From the moment the Order in Council [implementing Part IV of the Prices and Incomes Act] is made, the public is in these negotiations as a third party, as an interested party, and . . . when the powers become extinct next August the public interest will remain in the arguments about the level and distribution of income'. (*Report of the 65th Annual Conference of the Labour Party, Brighton 1966*, p. 213.)

direct self-government, but because the skills and techniques of modern administration need fairly specialized divisions of labour. In addition there are in Britain special local factors which emphasize the strength of the delgate's power. These are

1. *The strong element of élitism in political leadership,* discussed in Chapter III. The prominent members of both major parties are recruited from roughly the same strata and the same is increasingly true of the back-benchers. Leadership within the parties is highly centralized and backed by exceptionally strong discipline. Most of the senior civil servants, many of the top men in industry and finance and the professions share the background and the values of the political leaders; they communicate through a handful of quality media— *The Times, The Economist,* the BBC—which, at the higher reaches are also staffed by men largely like themselves. This does not mean that they are necessarily out of touch with the opinions of ordinary people: it does mean that they are a socially and intellectually unrepresentative, and relatively homogeneous, group. The similarity of background is largely provided by the equally élitist British educational system; in so far as this system is changing it could well lead to a fragmentation of the political élite, but it will clearly be some time before such a development can have a noticeable impact.

2. *The tradition of parliamentary independence,* discussed in Chapter I. Though this has its origins in the parliamentary struggle with the Crown and dates from the pre-reform era, the notion that parliament is a public forum, but nobody's servant, has survived virtually intact, largely thanks to the gradualness with which the franchise has been democratized. The mystique and ceremony of parliament help to keep it at one remove from mundane affairs.

3. *The collective character of political representation.* Once this was the direct representation of economic interests or family connections. For the past century the channelling of interest and opinion into workable units has been undertaken by party, so that today the conduct of elections and the working of parliament would be unthinkable without the party struggle.

It is in this inter-party competition that the voter can effectively intervene. A party enters an election in order to win a parliamentary majority; it wants a parliamentary majority in order to govern the country. There is only one, overriding issue in every British general election: the rival parties' fitness to govern. This is recognized by constitutional practice. Until 1868 it was customary for governments to resign only if defeated in a division in the House of Commons. In 1868 Disraeli set the precedent of resigning immediately it was obvious that he had lost the election. Because the choice is essentially between two parties many of the objections to the electoral method—

K

the irrationality of the voters, the difficulty of disentangling policy issues, the doubts surrounding the mandate theory—miss the point. General elections are useful for broad, not specific, decisions.

Two consequences flow from this, the first is that the personal qualities of the rival politicians, particularly the leaders of the two main parties, intrude very heavily into the campaigning. The second is that the party which is in power, and is therefore daily seen to be governing, has an advantage over the challenger. For the party in power, the art of political management consists of identifying itself, as far as possible, with a supra-partisan national interest. This is often referred to as 'consensus politics', though it is rarely clear whether this is to mean national agreement on specific topics or on ultimate aims (or both). To some extent this consensus, however defined, can be created or influenced by the government, in its choice of problems to tackle, and the way in which it decides to approach them. The party in power generally has the propaganda initiative, and it must try to use its leader's non-political position as head of the national administration to its full advantage. President Johnson exemplified the art of consensus-management when he told the citizens of Providence, Rhode Island, during the 1964 election campaign, 'We're in favour of a lot of things, and we're against mighty few'.[34] In Britain, analysis of the candidates' election addresses testifies to the special vote-getting power of the party leader when he is also Prime Minister. In 1964 41% of Conservative candidates mentioned Sir Alec Douglas-Home, while in 1966 only 19% mentioned Mr Heath; on the other hand the percentage of Labour candidates mentioning Mr Wilson rose from eight in 1964 to forty-seven in 1966.[35]

If it is the personality of the incumbent Prime Minister, and the administrative record of the outgoing government, that are really at stake in an election, then the parties start rather unevenly in the race. The plebiscite is not so much between equally poised rivals, as between rewarding or punishing the party in power. The onus of proving that he can govern better is laid on the challenger, and this is, in the nature of things, a difficult proposition to prove. Hence a government, however dim its record, can reckon on staying in power as long as its opponents do not inspire confidence; and to spend a lengthy period in opposition can in itself be a disadvantage, since it brings with it lack of administrative experience.

For Rousseau's objection to be valid, it would have to be shown that even if the voter can intervene effectively at election time, he cannot intervene effectively at any other time. But this, as should have emerged by now, is an untenable distinction. It is absurd to say to people: you may elect your leaders at intervals of five years, but you may not control, or are incapable of controlling, their actions during the intervals. For in that case the elections either do not impress the elected with a sense of public responsibility, which makes them pointless, or they do, in which case the public is involved at other times than the quinquennial consultations. In other words: *either* the British people are, in Rousseau's sense, 'free' even when elections are not taking place, *or* they are not free at all.

It is as a device for controlling political leaders that elections fulfil their most important function; it is by their effectiveness in doing so that their utility in British politics must in the last resort be judged. If they are effective, then the whole political culture is thereby transformed. Power, as a result, comes to be regarded as a trust, not as a right, and the politician's tenure of office as probationary, not permanent. The party struggle becomes a non-violent way of resolving a type of conflict which exists in all except the most primitive societies—the rivalry between different interests for state power. Elections become a non-violent way of solving a difficulty common to all political systems—how to organize the succession from one group of men holding authority to another. For this reason any electoral choice is better than none, even if the policy differences between the parties are trivial or their attitudes on major issues overlap. It is still worth-while to be able to choose between contestants of whom one is younger, or abler, or more honest than the other; indeed, it may be very important to be able to do so.

It has been argued earlier in this chapter that a political culture favourable to peaceful alternations of power is necessary before such a system can reliably function. It is equally true that the experience of reliable functioning reinforces public faith in the habits of tolerance and compromise. Political institutions and political manners are inseparable from each other as contributors to the characters of a régime. If this is true, we shall have to revise some of our earlier tentative conclusions. If elections are an effective control on political leaders, and are widely believed to be effective, then the voter does have an indirect influence on the content of the choice that he is given. Any party, whether in power or in opposition, which knows that it has to face an election within a given term of years, must take some trouble to draw up policies that look like being succcessful; and it will get rid of its leaders, often very ruthlessly, if their public rating sinks too far, as happened with Sir Alec Douglas-Home in the summer of 1965.

'No man could act with effect' thought Burke, 'who did not act in concert'.[36] All political choice, to be effective, has to be limited. In Britain it is limited to two major parties, highly disciplined, with loyal mass followings. At the same time the 'daily plebiscite' of public relations, policy statements and parliamentary debate keep the activities of the political élite in the public eye. The purpose of this activity is to urge the public to accept one of two rival leaderships; but the activity is necessary only because the final verdict is in the hands of the individual citizen. There can be no government by consent without the ritual of voting; and the right to vote periodically opens up countless indirect methods of expressing wishes and grievances at other times.

REFERENCES

CHAPTER V

1. Lane, R. E. & Sears, D. O. *Public Opinion* (Englewood Cliffs, N.J., 1964), p. 73.
2. Converse, P. E. & Dupeux, G. 'Politicisation of the Electorate in France and the United States', *Public Opinion Quarterly* XXVI (Spring, 1962), p. 9. Reprinted in: Campbell & others: *Elections and the Political Order*, p. 277.
3. Berelson, B. R. & others, *Voting*, pp. 311, 313.
4. Duncan, G. & Lukes, S. 'The New Democracy', *Political Studies* XI (June, 1963), p. 117.
5. *The Federalist*, No. 58, p. 253.
6. Quoted in *The Federalist*, No. 58, p. 254.
7. Mill, J. S. *Representative Government*, pp. 256-7.
8. *Ibid.*, p. 250.
9. Dahl, R. A. *A Preface to Democratic Theory*, p. 128.
10. *Ibid.*, pp. 129-30, 132.
11. Epstein, L. D. 'Electoral Decision and Policy Mandate: An Empirical Example', *Public Opinion Quarterly* XXVIII (Winter, 1964), p. 569. Cf. Milne & Mackenzie, *Straight Fight*, p. 139.
12. Quoted by Jennings, *Party Politics*, Vol. I, p. xiii.
13. Laprade, W. T. 'Public Opinion and the General Election of 1784', *English Historical Review* XXXI (April, 1916), pp. 224-37. George, Mrs E. 'Fox's Martyrs. The General Election of 1784', *Transactions of the Royal Historical Society*, 4th Series, XXI (1939), pp. 133-168.
14. Quoted by Nicolson, *People and Parliament*, pp. 97-8.
15. November 12, 1935, *H.C. Deb.*, 5th Series, vol. 317, 1105, quoted by Mowat, C. L. *Britain Between the Wars, 1918-1940* (London, 1955), p. 556.
16. Schumpeter, J. A. *Capitalism, Socialism and Democracy* (4th edn., London, 1954), p. 271.
17. *Ibid.*, p. 273.
18. Attlee, C. R. *The Labour Party in Perspective* (London, 1937), p. 93.
19. Williams, F. *A Prime Minister Remembers. The War and Post-War Memoirs of the Rt. Hon. Earl Attlee* (London, 1961), p. 91.
20. McKenzie, *British Political Parties*, p. 428, n. 1.

21. *Ibid.*, pp. 393, 627.
22. Quoted *ibid.*, pp. 615-6.
23. *Ibid.*, p. 204.
24. Quoted by Berkeley, H. 'Political Party Conferences', *The Listener*, September 22, 1966, p. 411.
25. Michels, R. *Zur Soziologie des Parteiwesens in der modernen Demokratie* (2nd edn., reprinted Stuttgart, 1957), pp. 138-9.
26. Jenkins, R. in: Rodgers, W. T. (ed.) *Hugh Gaitskell, 1906-1963* (London, 1964), p. 129.
27. McKenzie, *op, cit.*, p. 34.
28. Macleod, N. I. 'The Tory Leadership', *The Spectator*, January 17, 1964, p. 66.
29. Key, V. O., jr. *Public Opinion and American Democracy* (New York, 1961), p. 14.
30. Myrdal, G. *Beyond the Welfare State* (London, 1960), p. 33.
31. Beer, *Modern British Politics*, p. 30.
32. Beer, S. H. 'Pressure Groups and Parties in Britain', *American Political Science Review* L (March, 1956), p. 16.
33. Beer, *Modern British Politics*, p. 390.
34. White, T. H. *The Making of the President 1964* (London, 1965), p. 347.
35. Butler & King, *The British General Election of 1966*, p. 103.
36. Burke, E. 'Thoughts on the Cause of the Present Discontents', *Works*, Vol. II, p. 81.

BIBLIOGRAPHY

The following editions of standard classical texts have been used:

ARISTOTLE, *Politics*, translated with notes by Ernest Barker. Oxford University Press, 1948.

BAGEHOT, W. *The English Constitution*, with an introduction by R. S. H. Crossman, MP. The Fontana Library, Collins, London, 1962.

BURKE, E. *Works*. The World's Classics, 6 vols. Oxford Univerity Press, 1906–7.

HAMILTON, A., JAY, J. & MADISON, J. *The Federalist*. Everyman Library. J. M. Dent, London, 1911.

MICHELS, R. *Political Parties*. Introduction by Seymour Martin Lipset. The Free Press, Glencoe, 1962.

MILL, J. S. *Utilitarianism, Liberty and Representative Government*. Everyman Library. J. M. Dent, London, 1910.

ROUSSEAU, J-J. *Social Contract*. The World's Classics 511. Oxford University Press, 1947.

The following works are recommended for further reading. The titles of frequently cited periodicals have been abbreviated, viz.,

APSR – *American Political Science Review*
BJS – *British Journal of Sociology*
EHR – *English Historical Review*
PQ – *Political Quarterly*
PS – *Political Studies*

BACKGROUND READING

Constitutional:

BLONDEL, J. E. *Voters, Parties and Leaders. The Social Fabric of British Politics*. London, 1963.

KING, A. S. (ed.) *British Politics. People, Parties and Parliament*. New York, 1966.

MOODIE, G. C. *The Government of Great Britain*. 2nd edn. New York-London, 1964.

ROSE, R. *Politics in England*. London, 1965.

ROSE, R. (ed.) *Studies in British Politics. A Reader in Political Sociology*. London, 1966.

SMELLIE, K. B. *A Hundred Years of English Government*. 2nd edn. London, 1950.

Social and Cultural:

CARR-SAUNDERS, A. M., CARADOG-JONES, D. and MOSER, C. *Social Conditions in England and Wales*. Oxford, 1958.

GLASS, D. V. (ed.) *Social Mobility in Britain*. London, 1954.

HARRISON, J. F. C. *Society and Politics in England, 1780–1960.* New York, 1966.

HOGGART, R. *The Uses of Literacy.* London, 1957.

INGLIS, K. S. *Churches and the Working Classes in Victorian England.* London, 1963.

JACKSON B. & MARSDEN, D. *Education and the Working Class.* London, 1962.

RUNCIMAN W. G. *Relative Deprivation and Social Justice. A Study of Attitudes to Social Inequality in Twentieth-Century England.* London, 1966.

THE BRITISH REPRESENTATIONAL SYSTEM

History:

BLEWETT, N. 'The Franchise in the United Kingdom, 1885–1939.' *Past and Present*, 32. (December, 1965)

BUTLER, D. E. *The Electoral System in Britain since 1918.* 2nd edn. Oxford, 1963.

BUTLER, D. E. 'The Redistribution of Seats'. *Public Administration,* xxxiii (Summer, 1955)

BUTLER, J. R. M. *The Passing of the Great Reform Bill.* London, 1914.

DUNBABIN, J. P. D. 'Parliamentary Elections in Great Britain, 1858–1900: a Psephological Note.' *EHR*, LXXXI (January, 1966).

FOORD, A. S. *His Majesty's Opposition, 1714–1830.* Oxford, 1964.

GASH, N. *Politics in the Age of Peel. A Study in the Technique of Parliamentary Representation, 1830–50.* London, 1953.

HANHAM, H. J. *Elections and Party Management. Politics in the Time of Disraeli and Gladstone.* London, 1959.

JENNINGS, Sir Ivor. *Party Politics, I: Appeal to the People.* Cambridge, 1960.

LEONARD, R. L. *Elections in Britain.* Princeton-London, 1967.

LOWELL, A. L. *The Government of England.* 2nd edn. New York, 1926.

MORRIS, H. L. *Parliamentary Franchise Reform in England from 1885 to 1918.* New York, 1921.

NAMIER, Sir L. B. *England in the Age of the American Revolution.* 2nd edn. London, 1961.

NAMIER, Sir L. B. *The Structure of Politics at the Accession of George III.* 2nd edn. London, 1957.

NEALE, Sir J. E. *The Elizabethan House of Commons.* London, 1949.

PORRITT, E. & A. G. *The Unreformed House of Commons. Parliamentary Representation Before 1832.* Cambridge, 1903.

SEYMOUR, C. S. *Electoral Reform in England and Wales.* New Haven, 1915.

SMITH, F. B. *The Making of the Second Reform Bill*. Cambridge, 1966.

Election Results:

BUTLER, D. E. & FREEMAN, J. *British Political Facts, 1900–1960*. London, 1962.

MITCHELL, B. R. & BOEHM, K. *British Parliamentary Election Results, 1950–1964*. Cambridge, 1966.

TIMES, The [of London]. *Guide to the House of Commons*. London, 1918, 1929, 1931, 1935, 1945, 1950, 1951, 1955, 1959, 1964, 1966.

THEORIES OF REPRESENTATION

AMERY, L. S. *Thoughts on the Constitution*. Oxford, 1947.

BEER, S. H. *Modern British Politics*. London, 1965. [U.S.: *British Politics in the Collectivist Age*. New York, 1965]

BIRCH, A. H. *Representative and Responsible Government. An Essay on the British Constitution*. London, 1964.

BRYCE, Viscount. *Modern Democracies*. New York, 1924.

CHRISTOPH, J. B. 'Consensus and Cleavage in British Political Ideology.' *APSR* LIX (September, 1965)

DAHL, R. A. *A Preface to Democratic Theory*. Chicago, 1956.

DUNCAN, G. & LUKES, S. 'The New Democracy.' *PS* XI (June, 1963)

EPSTEIN, L. D. 'Electoral Decision and Policy Mandate: An Empirical Example.' *Public Opinion Quarterly*, XXVIII, Winter 1964.

GIBBONS, P. A. *Ideas of Political Representation in Parliament, 1651–1832*. Oxford, 1914.

MAY, J. D. 'Democracy, Organisation, Michels.' *ASPR* LIX (June, 1965)

MYRDAL, G. *Beyond the Welfare State*. London, 1960.

PLAMENATZ, J. & SARTORI, G. 'Electoral Studies and Democratic Theory.' *PS* VI (February, 1958)

RUNCIMAN, W. G. *Social Science and Political Theory*. Cambridge, 1963.

SCHUMPETER, J. A. *Capitalism, Socialism and Democracy*. 4th edn. London, 1954.

SCHATTSCHNEIDER, E. E. *Party Government*. New York, 1942.

ELECTION SURVEYS

British:

McCALLUM, R. B. & READMAN, A. *The British General Election of 1945*. Oxford, 1947.

NICHOLAS, H. G. *The British General Election of 1950*. London, 1951.

BUTLER, D. E. *The British General Election of 1951*. London, 1952.

BUTLER, D. E. *The British General Election of 1955*. London, 1955.

BUTLER, D. E. & ROSE, R. *The British General Election of 1959*. London, 1960.

BUTLER, D. E. & KING, A. S. *The British General Election of 1964*. London, 1965.

BUTLER, D. E. & KING, A. S. *The British General Election of 1966*. London, 1966.

BERRINGTON, H. B. 'The General Election of 1964.' *Journal of the Royal Statistical Society* Series A, CXXVIII (1965)

BERRINGTON, H. B .'The 1966 Election; An Analysis of the Results.' *Swinton Journal* XII (Autumn 1966)

BROMHEAD, P. 'The General Election of 1966.' *Parliamentary Affairs*, XIX (Summer 1966).

CRICK, B. 'Some Reflections on the Late Election.' *Public Law*, (Spring 1960)

KENDALL, M. G. & STUART, A. 'The Law of the Cubic Proportion in Election Results.' *BJS* I (September, 1950)

RASMUSSEN, J. S. 'The Disutility of the Swing Concept in British Psephology.' *Parliamentary Affairs* XVIII (Autumn, 1965)

Comparative:

CHAPMAN, R. M., JACKSON, W. K. & MITCHELL, A. V. *New Zealand Politics in Action. The 1960 General Election*. Oxford, 1962.

GOGUEL, F. and others. *Le Référendum d'Octobre et les Elections Législatives de Novembre 1962*. [Cahier de la Fondation Nationale des Sciences Politiques, 142] Paris, 1965.

KITZINGER, U. W. *German Electoral Politics. A Study of the 1957 Campaign*. Oxford, 1960.

RAWSON, D. W. *Australia Votes*. Melbourne, 1961.

WHITE, T. H. *The Making of the President, 1960*. London, 1961.

ELECTORAL SYSTEMS

CAMPBELL, P. W. *French Electoral Systems and Elections since 1789*. 2nd edn. London, 1965.

DUVERGER, M. (ed.) *L'Influence des Systèmes électoraux sur la Vie politique*. Paris, 1950.

HERMENS, F. A. *Democracy or Anarchy? A Study of Proportional Representation*. Notre Dame, 1941.

HOGAN, J. *Election and Representation*. Cork, 1945.

LAKEMAN, E. & LAMBERT, J. D. *Voting in Democracies. A Study of Majority and Proportional Electoral Systems*. London, 1955.

Ross, J. F. S. *Elections and Electors. Studies in Democratic Representation.* London, 1955.
Steed, M. 'Alternative Vote and Speaker's Conference.' *New Outlook* 49 (November-December, 1965)

POLITICAL PARTIES

British. Major Parties:
Attlee, C. R. *The Labour Party in Perspective.* London, 1937.
Bealey, F. & Pelling, H. *Labour and Politics, 1900–1906. A History of the Labour Representation Committee.* London, 1958.
Bulwer-Thomas, I. *The Growth of the British Party System.* London, 1965.
Burns, J. M. 'The Parliamentary Labour Party in Great Britain.' *ASPR*, xliv (September, 1950)
Cooke, G. W. *The History of Party. From the Rise of the Whig and Tory Factions in the Reign of Charles II to the Passing of the Reform Bill.* London, 1836–37.
Harrison, M. *Trade Unions and the Labour Party since 1945.* London, 1960.
Hoffman, J. D. *The Conservative Party in Opposition, 1945–51.* London, 1965.
Jennings, Sir Ivor. *Party Politics, II: The Growth of Parties.* Cambridge, 1961.
Lipson, L. 'The Two-Party System in British Politics.' *ASPR*, xlvii (June, 1953)
Macleod, I. N. 'The Tory Leadership'. *The Spectator* (London), January 17, 1964.
Miliband, R. *Parliamentary Socialism: A Study in the Politics of Labour.* London, 1961.
McKenzie, R. T. *British Political Parties.* 2nd edn. London, 1963.
Pelling, H. *The Origins of the Labour Party, 1880–1900.* 2nd edn. Oxford, 1965.
Rasmussen, J. S. *The Liberal Party. A Study of Retrenchment and Revival.* London, 1965.
Rose, R. 'Parties, Factions, and Tendencies in Britain.' *PS* xii (February, 1964)
Rose, S., McKenzie, R. T. & Miliband, R. 'Policy-Making in Opposition; Party Democracy and Parliamentary Government.' *PS* IV-V (June, 1956; June, 1957; June, 1958)
Trevelyan, G. M. *The Two-Party System in English Political History,* Romanes Lecture. Oxford, 1926.
Vincent, J. R. *The Formation of the Liberal Party, 1857–1868.* London, 1966.

WATKINS, A. *The Liberal Dilemma*. London, 1966.

British. Minor Parties, Regionalism:
BUDGE, I. S. & URWIN, D. W. *Scottish Political Behaviour. A Case Study in British Homogeneity.* London, 1966.
COUPLAND, Sir R. *Welsh and Scottish Nationalism. A Study.* London, 1954.
CROSS, C. *The Fascists in Britain.* London, 1961.
DOWSE, R. E. *Left in the Centre. The Independent Labour Party, 1893–1940.* London, 1966.
MORGAN, K. O. *Wales in British Politics, 1868–1922.* Cardiff, 1963.
PELLING, H. *The British Communist Party. A Historical Profile.* London, 1958.
THAYER, G. *The British Political Fringe. A Profile.* London, 1965.

Comparative:
DUVERGER, M. *Political Parties.* London, 1954.
ELDERSVELD, S. J. *Political Parties. A Behavioural Analysis.* Chicago, 1964.
EPSTEIN, L. 'British Mass Parties in Comparison with American Parties.' *Political Science Quarterly*, LXXI (March, 1956)
KEY, V. O., Jr. *Politics, Parties and Pressure Groups.* 5th edn. New York, 1964.
LEISERSON, A. *Parties and Politics. An Institutional and Behavioural Approach.* New York, 1958.
LOWELL, A. L. *Governments and Parties in Continental Europe.* Boston-New York, 1896.
NEUMAN, S. (ed.) *Modern Political Parties.* Chicago, 1956.
OSTROGORSKI, M. *Democracy and the Organisation of Political Parties.* London, 1902.

POLITICAL RECRUITMENT

BUCK, P. W. *Amateurs and Professionals in British Politics, 1918–59.* Chicago, 1963.
CRITCHLEY, J. & MAGEE, B. 'Candidates: How They Pick Them.' *New Statesman*, February 5, 1965.
GUTTSMAN, W. L. *The British Political Elite.* London, 1963.
McKITTERICK, T. E. M., REES-MOGG, W. & SKELSEY, P. 'Selection of Parliamentary Candidates.' *PQ* XXX (July, 1959).
MEYNAUD, J. & others. 'The Parliamentary Profession.' *International Social Science Journal* XXX/4 (1961)
RANNEY, A. *Pathways to Parliament. Candidate Selection in Britain.* London, 1965.

ROTH, A. *The Business Background of M.P.s* 5th edn. London, 1965.
WATT, D. 'Picking and Choosing.' *The Spectator*, May 1, 1964.

PARTY COHESION

British:
ALDERMAN, R. K. 'Discipline in the Labour Party, 1945–51.' *Parliamentary Affairs* XVIII (Summer, 1965)
BERKELEY, H. 'Party Political Conferences.' *The Listener*, September 22, 1966.
BLONDEL, J. 'The Conservative Association and the Labour Party in Reading.' *PS* VI (June, 1958)
DONNISON, D. and PLOWMAN, D. E. G. 'The Functions of Local Labour Parties: Experiments in Research Methods.' *PS* ii (June, 1954)
DOWSE, R. E. & SMITH, T. 'Party Discipline in the House of Commons.' *Parliamentary Affairs* XVI (Spring, 1963)
EPSTEIN, L. D. 'British M.P.s and their Local Parties: the Suez Cases.' *APSR* LIV (June, 1960)
EPSTEIN, L. D. 'New M.P.s and their Politics of the PLP.' *PS* x 2 (1962)
FIENBURGH, W., BIRCH, A. H., DONNISON, D. & JAHODA, G. 'Put Party Policy on the Agenda.' *Fabian Journal* 6 (February 1952)
FINER, S. E., BERRINGTON, H. B. & BARTHOLOMEW, D. J. *Backbench Opinion in the House of Commons, 1955–1959.* Pergamon Press, 1961.
HINDELL, K. & WILLIAMS, P. 'Scarborough and Blackpool: An analysis of Some Votes at the Labour Party Conferences of 1960 and 1961.' *PQ* XXXIII (July, 1962)
MARTIN, L. W. 'The Bournemouth Affair: Britain's First Primary Election.' *Journal of Politics*, XXII (November, 1960)
NICOLSON, N. *People and Parliament.* London, 1958.
POTTER, A. M. 'The English Conservative Constituency Associations.' *Western Political Quarterly* XI (June 1956)
RASMUSSEN, J. S. *The Relations of the Profumo Rebels with their Local Parties.* Tucson, Arizona, 1966.
RICHARDS, P. G. *Honourable Members.* London, 1959.
ROSE, R. 'The Policy Ideas of English Party Activists.' *APSR* LVI (June, 1962)

Comparative:
FROMAN, L. A. *Congressmen and their Constituencies.* Chicago, 1965.
McCLOSKY, H. and others. 'Issue Conflict and Consensus among Party Leaders and Followers'. *APSR* LIV (June, 1960)

PRESSURE GROUPS

British:
BEER, S. H. 'Pressure Groups and Parties in Britain.' *ASPR* L (March, 1956)
ECKSTEIN, H. *Pressure Group Politics* [The British Medical Association]. London, 1960.
FINER, S. E. *Anonymous Empire*. London, 1958.
McKENZIE, R. T. 'Parties, Pressure Groups and the British Political Process.' *PQ* XXIX (January, 1958)
POTTER, A. *Organised Groups in British National Politics*. London, 1961.
SELF, P. & STORING, H. *The State and the Farmer*. London, 1962.
STEWART, J. D. *British Pressure Groups*. Oxford, 1958.
WILSON, H. H. *Pressure Group. The Campaign for Commercial Television*. London, 1961.

Comparative:
EHRMANN, H. W. (ed.) *Interest Groups on Four Continents*. Pittsburgh, 1958.
MEYNAUD, J. *Les Groupes de Pression*. [Que Sais-Je? 895] Paris, 1960.
TRUMAN, D. B. *The Governmental Process*. New York, 1951.

SPECIAL ISSUES

CHRISTOPH, J. B. *Capital Punishment in British Politics*. London, 1962.
DRIVER, C. *The Disarmers. A Study in Protest*. London, 1965.
DEAKIN, N. D. (ed.) *Colour and the British Electorate, 1964*. London, 1965.
EPSTEIN, L. D. *British Politics in the Suez Crisis*. London, 1964.
SPIERS, M. & LeLOHE, M. J. 'Pakistanis in the Bradford Municipal Election of 1963.' *PS* XII (February, 1964)

VOTING BEHAVIOUR

British:
ABRAMS, M. 'Social Class and British Politics.' *Public Opinion Quarterly* XXV (Fall, 1961)
ALLEN, A. J. *The English Voter*. London, 1964.
BEALEY, F., BLONDEL, J. & McCANN, W. P. *Constituency Politics. A Study of Newcastle-under-Lyme*. London, 1965.
BENNEY, M., GRAY, A. P. & PEAR, R. H. *How People Vote*. [Greenwich]. London, 1956.

BIRCH, A. H. *Small-Town Politics*. [Glossop]. Oxford, 1959.
BIRCH, A. H. & CAMPBELL, P. W. 'Voting Behaviour in a Lancashire Constituency.' *BJS* I (September, 1950)
BONHAM, J. *The Middle-Class Vote*. London, 1954.
CAMPBELL, P. W., DONNISON, D. & POTTER, A. 'Voting Behaviour in Droylesden in October 1951.' *Manchester School of Economic and Social Studies* XX (January, 1952)
KAHAN, M., BUTLER, D. E. & STOKES, D. 'On the Analytical Division of Social Class.' *BJS* XVII (June, 1962)
MILNE, R. S. & MACKENZIE, H. C. *Straight Fight*. [Bristol, N-E] London, 1954.
MILNE, R. S. & MACKENZIE, H. C. *Marginal Seat* [Bristol N-E] London, 1958.
SAMUEL, R. 'The Deference Voter.' *New Left Review* No. 1. (Jan.-Feb., 1960)
STACEY, M. *Tradition and Change. A Study of Banbury*. Oxford, 1960.
VINCENT, J. R. *Pollbooks: How Victorians Voted*. Cambridge, 1967.
YOUNG, M. & WILLMOTT, P. 'Social Grading by Manual Workers.' *BJS* VII (December, 1956)

Comparative:
ALFORD, R. R. *Party and Society. The Anglo-American Democracies*. London, 1964.
ALMOND, G. A. & VERBA, S. *The Civic Culture. Political Attitudes and Democracy in Five Nations*. Abridged edn. Boston-Toronto, 1965.
BERELSON, B. R., LAZARSFELD, P. F. & McPHEE, W. N. *Voting. A Study of Opinion Formation in a Presidential Campaign*. Chicago, 1954.
CAMPBELL, A., CONVERSE, P. E., MILLER, W. E. & STOKES, D. E. *The American Voter*. New York, 1960.
CAMPBELL, A., CONVERSE, P. E., MILLER, W. E. & STOKES, D. E. *Elections and the Political Order*. New York, 1966.
LANE, R. E. *Political Life. Why and How People Get Involved in Politics*. 2nd edn. New York, 1964.
LAZARSFELD, P. F., BERELSON, B. & GAUDET, H. *The People's Choice. How the Voter Makes up his Mind in a Presidential Election*. 2nd edn. New York, 1948.
LIPSET, S. M. *Political Man*. New York, 1960.
MEYNAUD, J. & LANCELOT, A. *La Participation des Français à la Politique*. [Que Sais-Je? 911] 2nd edn. Paris, 1965.
MILBRATH, L. W. *Political Participation*. Chicago, 1965.
ROKKAN, S. & others. 'Citizen Participation in Political Life.' *International Social Science Journal* XII/1 (1960)

TINGSTEN, H. *Political Behaviour*. Stockholm, 1937.
SCHEUCH, E. K. & WILDENMANN, R. (eds.) 'Zur Soziologie der Wahl.' *Kölner Zeitschrift für Soziologie und Sozialpsychologie*. Sonderheft 9. Cologne, 1965.

POLITICAL COMMUNICATION AND
CAMPAIGN MANAGEMENT

British:
ABRAMS, M. 'Opinion Polls and Party Propaganda.' *Public Opinion Quarterly* xxviii (Spring, 1964)
ABRAMS, M. 'Why the Parties Advertise.' *New Society* June 6, 1963.
ABRAMS, M., ROSE, R. & HINDEN, R. *Must Labour Lose?* London, 1960.
BLUMLER, J. G. & McQUAIL, D. *Election Television in the 1960s.* London, 1967.
HARRISON, M. 'Political Finance in Britain.' *Journal of Politics* XXV (1963)
JENKINS, P. 'Labour's Election Machine.' *New Society*, May 28, 1964.
ROSE, R. *Influencing Voters. A Study of Campaign Rationality.* London, 1967.
ROSE, R. 'Money and Election Law.' *PS* IX (February, 1961)
TRENAMAN, J. & McQUAIL, D. *Television and the Political Image* [two Leeds constituencies] London, 1961.
WINDLESHAM, Lord. *Communication and Political Power.* London, 1966.

Comparative:
KELLEY, S. *Professional Public Relations and Political Power.* Baltimore, 1956.
KELLEY, S. *Political Campaigning. Problems in Creating an Informed Electorate.* Washington, D.C., 1960.
KEY, V. O. *Public Opinion and American Democracy.* New York, 1961.
LANE, R. E. & SEARS, D. O. *Public Opinion.* Englewood Cliffs, N.J., 1964.
NEWMAN, F. C. 'Money and Election Law in Britain—Guide for America.' *Western Political Quarterly* X (September, 1957)
WALLAS, G., *Human Nature in Politics.* London, 1908.

INDEX

L

Studies in Political Science

This is the first book in a new series consisting partly of special topics, such as 'The Making of Defence Policy' by J. A. Sabine, partly of studies epitomising wider areas, such as 'The Legislative Process' by S. A. Walkland. The series also falls into the two sections BRITISH GOVERNMENT and COMPARATIVE GOVERNMENT. It represents the tendency towards splitting the textbook so that each author is writing on the subject of his current interest or recent research, and it provides a platform for the younger generation of political scientists. Further early publications will be *The Prime Minister and the Cabinet* by J. P. Mackintosh, M.P., *'Politics and Planning'* by L. A. Gunn, *'The French Parliament 1958-1967'* by Philip Williams.